advance praise

"*Struck* is a beautiful testament to the magic ability we carry as humans to come together and heal from the most impossible wreckage. Douglas Segal's story moves your heart to break into a billion pieces and warms it back together with the brilliance, sincerity, and humor of his writing."

— Jill Soloway, creator of the Amazon show *Transparent* and author of *She Wants It*

"If love is the answer, the question is, how do I add more of it into my life? Susan and Doug's story of resilience teaches us not only how to survive life's biggest challenges, but how to make life worth living."

— Annabelle Gurwitch, author of *I See You Made an Effort* and *Wherever You Go, There They Are*

"This inspiring and heartwarming book underlines the importance of faith and love in the face of trauma."

— *Publishers Weekly*

"A powerful book that shows us a new way to look at incredible hardship. Being struck is not a tragic end, but rather a beginning: an opportunity to experience the awe-inspiring effects of love, community, and grit."

— Amy Silverstein, author of *Sick Girl* and *My Glory Was I Had Such Friends*

STRUCK

A Husband's Memoir of Trauma and Triumph

Douglas Segal

PROSPECT
·PARK·
BOOKS

Published by Prospect Park Books
2359 Lincoln Avenue
Altadena, CA 91001
www.prospectparkbooks.com

Distributed by Consortium Book Sales & Distribution
www.cbsd.com

**Library of Congress Cataloging in Publication Data is in process.
The following is for reference only.**
Names: Segal, Douglas, author.
Title: Struck: A husband's memoir of trauma and triumph / by Douglas
Segal.
Identifiers: ISBN 9781945551383 (pbk.) | ISBN 9781945551390 (ebook)
Subjects: Memoir

Cover design by David Ter-Avanesyan
Book layout and design by Amy Inouye, Future Studio

For Susan
I never wrote you a show,
but I did write you a book.

THE FIRST PART

the last day
of normal

The phone rings. I check the caller ID and don't recognize it; I'm not going to answer. I've got twenty-five minutes before I have to get on a conference call with Disney, and before that, I want to rewrite a couple of lines of a television pilot I'm delivering today.

But the phone continues to ring. I wait for the answering machine to get it, but for some godforsaken reason, it's not picking up. I exhale, annoyed because I know the call is either going to be for Susan (she's the only one who receives calls on the home line, and she left to take Alyce to school ten minutes ago) or it's the latest of 300 recent attempts to sell me something I have absolutely no interest in. Because of the persistent ringing and the malfunctioning answering machine, I'm going to have to answer it.

"Hello," I say, an edge in my voice.

The reply on the other end surprises me.

"Daddy, it's me." It's Alyce, my twelve-year-old daughter, her sweet yet scared voice on the other end. But why is she calling from this strange number, and worse, why is she crying and why does she sound so frightened?

"Mommy was just in a car accident."

My heart stops...and then immediately begins pounding.

"Are you all right?"
"Yes."
"Is Mommy?"
Another deep sob.
"I don't know...I don't think so. Come quick."

We're all familiar with the saying "There but for the grace of God go I." On this particular October morning, that grace was gone...and it was I.

the
news breaks

Word of the accident spread faster than the typical hyper-speed of Hollywood gossip. To be fair, though, this was a far cry from gossip. In addition to our friends informing one another, our temple's entire congregation had been notified through an email blast, and the collective response was one of sincere concern from a deeply caring community. Everyone recognized the randomness of the event, and because it happened so close to the temple where many of them sent their children to school, they also recognized how easily something like this could happen to them.

Again, there but for the grace of God...

What's inherent in that statement, though, is something I have grappled with from the very beginning: What role, if any, did some omnipotent being play in all of this? Did God really have anything to do with the accident? Which leads to several other equally unanswerable questions: Are there really any "accidents," or do things happen for a reason? Is this all some sort of life lesson that we should be learning from a very *bad* thing happening to *good* people? With this kind of event, it's unrealistic to not at least contemplate the big question of "Why?" even while simultaneously knowing it's a futile exercise. Still, sitting there in the hospital, waiting and wondering and worrying while life hung in the balance, it's impossible to not be slapped in the face by it.

Regardless, it quickly became impossible to process this in solitude. The "news" was out there, through that initial email as well as on all the local television stations. Because of the huge circle of friends Susan has built in her life, I almost immediately began receiving calls asking what was going on, what her condition was, was she going to be okay? There was so much uncertainty, though, that I didn't know what to say other than, "It's not good."

Things were far from stable, her condition as well as my emotional state. It wasn't so much what the doctors were telling me, but rather what they weren't, things they were leaving out, details and prognoses I still don't know and am probably better off never knowing. There was inside knowledge, that awful truth, and then there was me, blissfully ignorant to it all.

I don't blame the doctors for keeping their secrets. I already had enough to worry about that was *real*, never mind working myself into a state of panic over *possibilities*. It would be too easy to spin myself crazy indulging in all the "mights" of the situation (if she survives "this," she *might* then be faced with "that"—the "thats" being paralysis, brain damage, etc.). So not knowing the possibilities was a layer of protection necessary to deal with the immediate, to focus on the present.

This is a great lesson I learned right out of the gate from the emergency room doctors and nurses. They aren't concerned with the past or the future. Their complete focus and attention is right there in the moment, on that body in front of them. Nothing else matters. And as I sat in the ICU waiting room, I tried to remain in that same state of present.

Even in these earliest hours, I was never alone. In addition to my group of friends, there were others in the waiting room, people I didn't know who were related to other patients on the floor. We shared hellos, offering some of the mountain of food that had been delivered to us from other concerned friends. We exchanged sympathetic, unspoken looks acknowledging that we'd rather be anywhere else than where we were, and that though strangers, we were bound by unrelated illness or tragedy.

The images of the accident were not only haunting my memory, they remained right in front of me, broadcast all over the news. I'd catch glimpses on the television in the background, repeating the footage. But I didn't need to see it again.

At one point, a man caught a look at the accident on the TV and innocently remarked to me, "Wow, look at that accident on Hollywood Boulevard. Miracle if anyone survived that. You gotta take a look at this."

I politely declined. He pressed again for me to check it out. "No, seriously, this is unbelievable!"

The man's wife nudged him and whispered under her breath. I knew exactly what she was saying without having to hear it.

His face turned pale before he turned to me, apologizing. "I didn't know. I'm sorry."

I told him not to worry about it. I knew he was just innocently trying to distract me from whatever I was going through. But what was interesting was that in that one moment, the sensational news story about some random stranger had become personal for him. In that instant, he realized that in that car, behind this crazy news story, was a very real person with a husband, children, friends, and family who were all waiting in this very room, and like him, concerned whether their loved one was going to live or die. As with any accident or disaster, that awareness, that personal connection, makes the story a lot less fascinating to simply casually watch. It humanizes it.

By this point, the waiting room had also become like central operations for a major campaign headquarters. A circle of five or so women, all Susan's closest friends, were gathered in a circle, laptops clacking away. Meal trains were being formed, friends were being updated with the latest news, carpools were being organized. It was an efficient, progesterone-charged power machine. I looked around at them and commented, "God, if we could harness what's going on in this waiting room right now, I am quite confident we could solve all of the world's problems."

It was true. The amount of focus, care, and energy was unstoppable.

I sat there, primarily in a daze, holding in my hand the hospital turkey sandwich a nurse had given me for Alyce hours earlier in the emergency room. At the time, Alyce didn't want it and neither did I. Every few minutes someone would remind me that I really should eat something (it's not like we had any shortage of food), but I had been trying to lose some weight over the past few months, doing the whole no-carb, lean-protein thing, and I hadn't consumed a piece of bread in some time. I sat there looking at this sandwich. Should I eat it? Was this really just a sandwich, or was it a parable for a bigger test from God? Did this turkey sandwich represent my strength, and if I gave in and ate it, was that giving up? It was now much bigger than just a sandwich; it was my ability to handle this crisis. It was absurd and ridiculous, but these are the kinds of things you think about, or at least I was thinking about.

As the day wore on, I was approached by a friend who gently suggested (again) that I really needed to put out some kind of statement, like a diplomat following a horrific public event. The team was being overwhelmed with phone calls, emails, and texts, and the consensus was that I needed to reach out and provide some information. Visitors weren't allowed into the building, never mind onto our floor of the ICU, unless I put them on a list. As a result, there were so many who felt shut out, both literally and figuratively.

But I felt strongly that I didn't want to provide any specific information about Susan's injuries until I had a clear understanding of what they were myself. As far as I was concerned, no information was better than false information. I also didn't want to speculate, even from a place of optimism, that she was going to be okay, partly because I didn't know and partly because I didn't want to jinx it by making that declaration. I had experienced this exact situation earlier while I was in the ER with Alyce, heartened by Susan's initial positive prognosis, only to have the doctors reverse it just moments later. I could tell that this was the way it was going to be, good news followed by terrible followed by better...constantly changing. It was hard enough for me to go on this ride, and, whether right or wrong, I didn't want to drag anyone else onto this hellish roller coaster.

Yet, there were too many people in our lives who were in the dark, and I know that the dark can be a scary place to be, full of uncertainty and anxiety.

And it wasn't only *what* to say but *where* to say it. I ultimately chose Susan's Facebook page, figuring that would reach the majority of her friends, and if someone wasn't a Facebook friend, then they would hear it from someone who was. I also realized that there would be many around the country with no knowledge of the accident who would read the post and wonder what the hell was going on. There was no perfect way to say it—not in words or format—but in this world of social networking, it seemed like the most efficient way to get information out as quickly, and to as many, as possible.

Early evening, albeit brief, this is what I posted on her page:

Susan Segal
October 23, 2012, near Los Angeles, CA

Hi, everyone, it's Doug. I want to thank you all for your thoughts and prayers, and I will try to keep you updated on the situation. The hospital staff and Susan have a great challenge ahead of them, but I, and Susan, know she is surrounded by love, and we all so very much appreciate your concern. With much love and gratitude to the amazing support and friends we both have. xxoo, d

Even though I had written that Susan knew she was "surrounded by love," I wouldn't realize the full extent of that until much later on. There have been recent studies that show that this kind of energy translates to whomever it's intended, whether the "giver" is present in the room of the "receiver" or not. It is this love, support, compassion, and prayer that became Susan's lifeblood, transferred through some cosmic transfusion.

As the hours ticked by, we all mostly just sat, interminably waiting for news. Good news would be met with a surge of energy and relief, while no news (which was more often the case) was met with quiet frustration. As night began to fall, the number of calls, texts, and emails continued to flood in from family and friends asking to please be notified if there was any further news. One friend became the gatekeeper of this contact list as the constant influx of people made it too much for me to keep track of.

And so at the close of the first day, I wrote the first of what became known as the "updates." At first, the updates began as a way to keep our family and friends informed about Susan's physical condition, but they quickly grew to become much more than just a clinical recounting of her recovery. Yes, they told that story, but as she wrestled for her life, everyone receiving the updates wrestled with the life questions and issues that the accident raised—like me, trying to make sense of what ultimately makes no sense.

I could count up the email addresses on the master list, but that wouldn't come close to providing an accurate number of actual recipients, as there were many on the list who forwarded them on to others—their parents, friends, family, workmates, and countless others, many of whom didn't even know me or Susan but were so moved by the randomness and the heartbreak of the accident that they wanted to be kept abreast, to remain a part of it.

I always felt that everyone who wanted to continue to receive the updates truly cared, was moved, and in many cases later shared how they were inspired by them. For many who would read our story, we were like fictional characters in an ongoing serial, but at the same time, it was impossible to ignore that we were also real people, people just like them, and that is what connected and moved them.

Ultimately, I didn't need to know who they were. The real hope was, since they were now plunged into this journey with us, that they, too, would be sending their love and support.

I didn't need to know anything more than that.

day 1

As you know, Susan and Alyce were involved in a terrible car accident this morning. Alyce is thankfully okay, but Susan has been very seriously injured.

I am still waiting for news about her condition, which as you can imagine is constantly changing given the scope of her injuries.

Please know that I deeply appreciate all your concern, prayers, and warm thoughts and will convey them as soon as I am able to see her. I will also send more definitive updates as soon as I have more information.

a little bit
of backstory

S ince this whole saga is a love story of sorts, it probably makes sense to get to know the main characters a little better.

Susan and I met around Thanksgiving in 1988. We both lived in New York City, actually quite near each other. As we would learn, this was just one of the many coincidences we shared.

Earlier in the day of the night we met, I had gotten a call from a college friend of mine, Geoffrey. He told me that he and a friend from his acting class were going up to a party that night and, knowing I had just gotten out of a relationship, asked if I'd like to join them. I didn't have anything going on, so I said yes. The plan was to meet at the Cooper Square subway station and head to the party from there. They would be coming from a show at the Public Theatre.

His friend was Susan.

As we took the subway up to the party, they told me about this avant-garde play they had just seen, laughing about how very little of it made sense to them. I hadn't seen the show, but I had seen a lot of experimental theater, so I offered my analysis. Susan would later say that her first thought about me was that I was smart, hearing me analyze this crazy play. I remember thinking at the time that for my next relationship, I wanted to find someone like her. She was smart, funny, pretty, with a mane of curly hair and bright blue eyes, and an equally attractive, strong personality. She spoke her mind unapologetically, verbalizing thoughts most of us have but aren't brave enough to express. This, I learned, was a quality most would love about her, though on occasion, some would find abrasive and be put off. In any case, I was really happy for Geoffrey. He seemed to have found himself a really great girl.

That party was fairly uneventful in terms of *our* future relationship, but a couple of weeks later, we found ourselves at another one. Geoffrey and Susan were presumably still a couple, which I was happy to see, but at the party, Susan and I found ourselves spending most of the time together. It wasn't our riveting conversation that kept us rooted in the same spot; it was the loaf of Zabar's cinnamon babka (a kind of coffee cake/bread), which we devoured together. It was gooey and cinnamony and irresistibly delicious, and we continued to cut slice after slice of it. As we stuffed our faces, we managed to get a few words in here and there. I asked her where she was from, and she said, "Massachusetts."

"Me, too," I responded, surprised. "What part?"

"Framingham?" she said, wondering if I'd ever heard of it.

Of course I'd heard of it. "My uncle and aunt live in Framingham."

"Really? What are their names?"

"Joan and Bob Smith?"

I posed it as a question because the likelihood that Susan would know my uncle and aunt from what is considered the largest town in the United States was remote, never mind ones with the name Smith.

"Bob Smith the dentist?"

"Yeah!" (He was actually an oral surgeon, but I figured she was talking about the same one.)

"Oh, my God, they're dear friends of my parents—"

"No kidding?"

"—who for years have been telling me that they have a nephew I would really like!"

(Needless to say, there were no happier people at our wedding than Joan and Bob Smith, who were proud to proclaim to everyone, "We knew it!")

After spending most of the night talking (and eating), I unintentionally gave Susan my best and only pickup line ever. "You know, you'd be perfect for a musical I want to write."

It actually was true. I was in the early stages of writing a show that featured a Bette Midler–like character, and that was Susan...brassy, sexy. She really was perfect. I told her a little about the idea, which, naturally, since I would be writing it for her, she loved. Twenty-five years later, she's still waiting for me to write that show.

As the night wore on, Geoffrey and Susan were ready to go home. We all lived near one another in the East Village, so they urged me to leave with them and share a cab downtown. However, I wasn't so sure I wanted to go just yet. Though I really loved talking to Susan that night, she was leaving with Geoffrey, and there were some other possible prospects at the party. They persisted, insisting I join them, and ultimately I relented.

We got into a cab, Susan sitting between us, and as we drove downtown, I rested my hand on my right thigh. Susan's hand was resting on her left thigh, and lo and behold, our hands just happened to touch. I remember thinking that I should move my hand from its illicit position, but I didn't. We weren't exactly holding hands, but I was very aware of the electricity of the touch, and it was exciting. But I also felt extremely guilty. Geoffrey was one of my best friends, and here I was having a secret hand affair with his girlfriend.

We eventually reached our destination, and I said an awkward goodbye, not knowing when or if I would see Susan again. However, shortly thereafter, Geoffrey moved to Los Angeles, and just after New Year's, I returned home from work to find a message from Susan on my answering machine. It went kind of like this...

"Hi, it's Susan Roffer, Geoffrey's friend. I just spoke to Geoffrey, who says that since we live so close to each other, we should hang out sometime."

Interesting. *Geoffrey* suggested we should hang out? Maybe they weren't together after all. I called Susan back that night, which I later learned freaked her out because I responded so quickly. I didn't wait a day or three or whatever the appropriate amount of time to convey *I'm not desperate* is. Truth is, I didn't even think about giving it a couple of days before I responded. One thing I had learned by that point in my life was to go for the things I wanted, especially when it came to romance. If a woman said no, then so be it; at least I'd know and could move on. If she said yes, then, great, more time we'd have in our lives to be together.

During the phone call, I asked Susan out for that weekend, but she said she had plans on Saturday night to see a play. She was going with another friend, but then asked me if I'd like to join them. When I told her that I didn't want to intrude on her date, she insisted that it was "just a friend." To her surprise, I think, I accepted.

That Saturday I met her at the theater and saw one of the worst plays I've ever seen in my life. It was a tiny production, so poorly attended that there were more people on the stage than in the audience. One of the actors was a little boy, who when he made his entrance, walked to the edge of the stage and began waving and mouthing "Hi, Mommy" to his mother in the audience. It truly was painful.

Quite the opposite from the agonizing performance was being there with Susan. The theater was freezing inside, so the two of us sat watching the show with our feet up on the seats in front of us, snuggled underneath her massive down coat. It was definitely a testament to the notion that it really doesn't matter how miserable what you're doing is as long as you're doing it with someone you enjoy.

After the play, Susan's friend politely excused himself and left. I'm not sure whether this had been set up between the two, with some sort of signal planned for him to bail if things were going well or to absolutely not leave her alone with me if things sucked. In any case, we were now on our own, and since we lived so close to each other, I asked her if she wanted to have a post-theater dinner in the neighborhood. She was into that, and so we had a plan.

It had begun to snow—big fluffy flakes, unusual for New York. If someone had been production-designing the date, they couldn't have done it more romantically. The streets were fairly empty as we hailed a cab and climbed inside. Now, I usually hate cabs because of the crazy, erratic driving, but on this night, we lucked out. We had Radu as a driver, and whether it was the heavy snow falling or just his personal philosophy, he was in no hurry to get anywhere and neither were we. Maybe he sensed that in the back seat of his cab were two young lovers, clearly enjoying life and being together. We laughed most of the way to our destination, and when we arrived, Radu did something no other cab driver had ever done before or since. He turned toward us in the back seat, clasped his hands together, and with a big smile said, "Bless you both."

This was the first of our blessings.

Eight months later we were engaged, and seven months after that we were married. A year into marriage, we decided to pack up our newly purchased Honda Accord and drive out to Los Angeles to give the movie business a shot. We gave ourselves a *whole* month to make it. We very soon realized that this was a ridiculously short amount of time and that, instead, we would give it a year. If nothing came of it, we'd figure something else out.

For the next few years, we did all right. I was able to break into the movie business, working in development and growing into a producer on such films as *Cool Runnings, City of Angels*, and *Three Kings*. Susan had landed guest parts on pretty much every sitcom, including *Seinfeld, Murphy Brown, Everybody Loves Raymond*, and *Curb Your Enthusiasm*. When she shot *Everybody Loves Raymond*, she was very pregnant with our next blessing, Michael, and when she appeared in *Curb*, she was very pregnant with the blessing that followed Michael: Alyce.

For the most part, our cab driver Radu had called it: We've been pretty blessed. Married for more than twenty years—and that's Hollywood years, which has a multiplier even greater than for dogs' lives—with two beautiful and healthy children. Was our marriage perfect? I guess I'd like to know what that looks like. After all, with any marriage, regardless of its length, come the usual aggravations. In those twenty years, we had both come to know very well how to push each other's buttons, and on occasion, those buttons definitely got pushed. Sometimes we'd fight on point, addressing real issues, which basically could be narrowed down to either taking each other for granted or not treating each other with respect. Other times we'd just fight, letting the stresses of life spill into our relationship.

More recently, the responsibility of financially carrying the family on my shoulders had taken its toll, and beyond that, I had been feeling that my overall role in the household was disproportionate to Susan's, that in order to get things done right, I had to do them myself. This resulted in a load of resentment, which then led to fights over the pettiest of things. A typical rant of mine might center on the all-important dishwasher. "You know what would be great? If you could just take two extra seconds and rinse the dishes and not just pile them in on top of each other; then maybe they'd actually get clean instead of the food getting baked onto them, which then takes me like twenty times longer to get off instead of those two little seconds. That would be *super* helpful!" Without a degree in psychology, I'm guessing that these blowups weren't exactly about the loading of the dishwasher.

And while after twenty years we often still made each other laugh, there was plenty that caused conflict. From her point of view, I picked on her, didn't appreciate her, tell her I love her enough, compliment her appearance enough—pretty basic male stuff that I confess to be guilty of. My issues generally centered around laziness or selfishness, or that it often felt to me like her relationships with her phone and computer were more passionate and involved than ours.

Then, of course, there's the money...or lack of it. I've done okay in my years and overall have been pretty fortunate, but it's been a struggle, and however much I have earned has never been quite enough to support our nut and lifestyle. Susan's work as an actress had become intermittent at best, and while she did begin teaching a Parent and Me class, it didn't make a significant financial contribution toward our expenses. We found ourselves slipping further and further into debt, borrowing against the house we own. I saw the direction we were headed, knowing that at this rate something was going to have to change, which led to more fights—fights about my career and what I wasn't doing to further it, who I wasn't calling or schmoozing. Now granted, her point of view was usually from a place of support; she didn't understand why I wasn't more successful, given that I was so talented. But it didn't always feel supportive. It also didn't really reflect an understanding of the business, the luck of it, the randomness of it. Years of being a freelancer had forced me to develop—or at least try to develop—a sense of Zen about my career. I lived on faith that it would all work out, and up to this point, it had. I'd been able to hang on, even though sometimes, especially lately, it felt like it was by the skin of my teeth.

And so, as with most long-term relationships, I suppose, there was enough stress, conflict, and dissatisfaction to consider...alternatives. Divorce, though, has never really been on the table. I had taken an oath—for better, for worse, for richer, for poorer, in sickness and in health. It just wasn't an option I ever entertained. No affairs either. Over the years, especially in this business, there were most likely opportunities had I pursued them, but still I remained true.

However, it would be a lie to say that I never wondered about what it would be like if the marriage were to end in some other way, by something I had no control over—like a plane crash or a sudden disease, maybe something quick like a heart attack or aneurism. (I didn't need her to suffer; that would just be cruel.) In these scenarios, I would suddenly become the tragic widower, garner caring sympathy, which would eventually lead to meeting someone new, falling in love, experiencing the excitement of a blossoming relationship again. A fresh start, a new chapter, a do-over. During our marriage, I'd seen it happen to others, spouses who died of cancer and their surviving partners finding new love. I'd also witnessed friends who judged these burgeoning relationships with disdain. But my assessment of their disgust wasn't that they were disapproving of the new relationship as much as that they were jealous, envious that this "lucky" person got to shed the dead skin of their old relationship and find something fresh and exciting while they remained stuck. And, yes, as ugly as it sounds, I do confess to, on the rare occasion, letting that perverted romantic fantasy, the one driven by the hand of God rather than by personal choice, play in my head.

Who knew that I was about to be confronted head-on with the possibility of that fantasy becoming a reality? Yet, when that reality presented itself, I was instantly reminded of all the good that would be ripped away—the comfort, the laughter, the support, the friendship...the love. The forgotten foundation of our marriage. And in that moment, there was absolutely nothing romantic or "lucky" about the fantasy. It was only just painfully and terrifyingly tragic.

day 2: the beginning of the day

Dear friends,

The outpouring of love, support, healing thoughts, and prayers from all of you is so appreciated. I always knew Susan and I were blessed to have such wonderful friends, but until something like this happens, it's hard to really fathom the scope. I know there are a lot of questions about Susan's condition, and unfortunately, until things settle down it's best that I simply say that we're hoping and praying for the best possible outcome. As you know, there's no one stronger than Susan, and she knows how loved she is.

Again, thank you all for your ongoing concern and support. It is appreciated more than you know.

With much love,
Doug

that unforgettable day: parts 1 & 2

It was just after 10 p.m. when I crawled into bed for the night.

I remember the time because it was the earliest I'd gone to bed in months. Since the summer, I had been juggling a number of projects: I was in post-production on a movie I had written and produced, finishing a writing assignment for Disney, plus writing the new *Tom and Jerry* cartoon, all in the middle of post-production on a new unscripted TV show I was running and finishing a pilot I had sold to the CW. So for some time, I had been busy, really busy, but all in a good way.

After turning my phone off for the night, I turned to Susan and said, "Wow, for the first time in I don't know how long, I'm all caught up. I'm delivering my rewrite tomorrow, and other than that, everything else is done." She was congratulating me when I added, "But I have a conference call with Disney tomorrow morning, so do you think you could take Alyce to school?"

"Sure," she replied. "No problem."

Generally, our routine was that she would get up early

and take Michael, who was a freshman in high school, to his bus stop before she went to the Y to work out. I'd get up an hour later, take Alyce to school, and then head to work. The schedule usually worked out pretty well, but on this day, she'd have to miss her workout so that I could take my conference call. The good news for me was, since I didn't have to take Alyce to school, I could sleep a little later and shower before my call.

You know the next part. About how I got up to do a little work before my conference call. About how the phone rang and for some reason, the answering machine didn't pick up. About how I picked up the phone (and so lucky that I did) and heard Alyce's scared and crying voice on the other end.

"Daddy, it's me...Mommy was just in a car accident."

"Are you all right?"

"Yes."

"Is Mommy?"

"I don't know...I don't think so. Come quick."

"Where are you?"

"On Hollywood Boulevard, right by the house."

"Okay, I'll be right there."

"No, you need to come now!"

I realized the way I'd said "I'll be right there" was interpreted as a typical response I might have given her. "Daddy, can you come here and help with my homework?" and I'd say "Yeah, I'll be right there" while I finished whatever I was working on. Like, in this case, I was going to finish my work, hop in the shower, maybe have a little bite to eat before finally getting around to checking out the accident.

"Yes, I'm coming right now. Don't move."

"Okay. I love you," she sobbed.

I jumped up, pulled on some clothes, and was sprinting out the door in about thirty seconds. As I left the house, I looked over at the answering machine in the kitchen and saw that it wasn't on at all. Strange.

By the time I pulled out, I could already tell traffic was being diverted down the side streets around our house in order to circumvent the accident. And like a bumper car going the wrong direction against the flow, I headed toward the mess rather than away from it.

I turned east on Hollywood Boulevard and could see what looked like a film shoot for a disaster movie just a couple of blocks away. The street was completely blocked off; fire engines, police cars, and ambulances were randomly parked in the middle of the street; helicopters circled in the sky. I still couldn't see the actual accident, so I drove toward the mayhem while everyone else was doing whatever they could to avoid it.

Reaching the point where the street was blocked off, I turned left up a side street and miraculously found a parking spot. I jumped out of the car, ran down Hollywood Boulevard, approached the scene...and that's when I saw it. A city bus was parked going the wrong direction on the far right-hand side of the street. And in front of it were the smashed remains of Susan's BMW. It literally looked as though the bus was trying to devour it, the front end of the car completely consumed—either not visible or nonexistent. I couldn't tell.

My hand immediately went to my mouth, and I remember uttering out loud, "Oh, fuck."

I couldn't even comprehend the scene. What was the bus doing on the wrong side of the street? Every way I looked at this, I couldn't see what Susan could have done to contribute to this bizarre configuration. This was not the first of her accidents, but they usually fell into the category of an "oops" involving immovable objects like signs, dumpsters, garages, bicycles, concrete posts....

"Where'd the scrape on your bumper come from?"

"Oh, I backed into a dumpster." And then she'd give me a guilty little smile...oops.

"How'd you get that dent in the trunk?"

"Oh, I backed into a post."

My favorite driving story of Susan's, though, if I can digress from the main drama for a minute more, was when she was a teenager and worked at Hickory Farms in Shopper's World in Massachusetts. She was leaving work for the day, got into her dad's gigantic Pontiac, backed up, and started heading toward the exit onto Route 9. As she was driving through the parking lot, she looked in her rearview mirror and saw a VW bug right behind her, the driver waving her hand. Susan didn't immediately recognize who it was but gave her a friendly wave back, figuring it was someone she knew, and then continued on to the exit. A couple hundred yards farther on, she again looked in the rearview and saw the same woman behind her, still waving, now a little more frantically. Susan thought it was strange that this woman was following so closely behind her, but she nevertheless continued on until she was just about to turn onto busy Route 9. That's when the woman behind her began leaning on her horn. Susan finally stopped the car and got out to find out what was going on. The woman jumped out of her car and shouted, "Your trailer hitch hooked onto my bumper when you backed out of your parking space! You've been towing me around!" Susan looked at the two cars, and sure enough they were connected. Oops.

However, there was no oops to this accident, and looking at it even from fifty yards away, I couldn't conceive how anyone could have possibly survived it.

I immediately searched the area for Alyce and finally

saw her on the corner of the street amid a number of pass-ersby and bus passengers. She was standing there crying, a stranger comforting her.

I ran up to her and pulled her into my arms. As she bur-ied her head into my chest, sobbing, I looked beyond her to the car and thought, *Oh, my God, how is she even still alive?* She was covered in tiny shards of glass, in her hair, on her clothes, but uninjured...and she had been in the front seat! I held onto her, unable to believe the miracle of her. I remem-ber thinking, *Am I really holding on to my baby girl? Or have I gone crazy and she's actually still in the front seat of the car and I've slipped into some other reality where my brain created this alternative universe, unable to cope with having lost her?* I held her tighter. Still, I couldn't imagine if I had run up to this horrific scene and found her body, limp in the front seat of the accordioned car.

I brushed the glass and tears off her cheeks, bent down, and asked her if she was okay. Did she hurt anywhere? She shook her head no.

Inconceivable.

As I held her, I could see the emergency crew cutting the roof off the car to reach Susan, still trapped in its crum-pled frame.

"Wait right here, baby, okay? I want to go check on Mommy."

She nodded, still crying, afraid of what I was going to find in the driver's seat.

I let go of her and walked toward the car. As I approached, I first saw the passenger side, the deflated air bag, the de-stroyed interior, the door completely popped off, strewn on the sidewalk. I again shook my head in disbelief that Alyce had walked away from this.

And then I saw Susan inside.

She was conscious, but pinned under the dashboard

and steering wheel, her air bag also deployed and deflated. There was no front windshield—there was no front end, for that matter—but by some miracle she was conscious and reaching with her left arm for someone to help her. There was some blood on the air bags, but I couldn't see the source. Honestly, I couldn't see much of anything.

She blindly called out for someone to help her, anyone, her eyes not focused. I shouted to her, but she couldn't hear me. I yelled again, but I was too far away. I tried to move closer to let her know I was there, but a policeman or paramedic held me back. "You need to clear the area, sir."

And that was my cue to recite my line in this surreal movie scene. "I'm her husband."

The officer was compassionate but continued to usher me away. Susan still didn't know I was there, didn't know Alyce was okay. She was alone in her hell, and I was helpless.

I returned to Alyce, who asked if Mommy was okay. I told her that I didn't know but that she was conscious, so that was a good sign. And then I looked down at my watch. It was 8:25; my conference call was due to start in five minutes, not that I intended to be on it. I remember thinking as I dialed the phone, the absurdity that Disney would be the first call I made regarding the accident, not family or friends. Disney.

My producer answered the phone, and I began to shakily speak. "Dave, it's Doug. Listen, my wife was just in a car accident, so I won't be able to make the call."

"Oh, okay, no problem," he replied. Thankfully, he didn't press for any details, just continued, "We'll let you know how it goes. Hope she's okay."

"Thanks," I responded and hung up. With my phone still in hand, I thought, 'I should take a picture of this...to be able to identify the bus and document the scene. Even though it was for good reason, I still felt guilty for taking a picture—

that somehow I was exploiting the situation. How could I be thinking of making business calls and snapping pictures at the scene of my wife's accident? It was all so confusing, so I only took the one photo.

Later, when I asked Alyce what she remembered about the accident, one of the things she told me was that when she got out of the car, she saw a river of blood running down the street. I'm pretty sure it was engine coolant, but it's easy to see why she would think that from this scene of horror.

My phone buzzed. From the caller ID I could see it was Tracy, our former neighbor, who lived right around the corner from the accident. I answered, and all I got out was "Hi" before she immediately began speaking.

"I'm watching the news. Please tell me that's not Susan. Tell me that's not her in the car."

I really wished I could have been able to say it wasn't, but, instead, through tears I confessed, "It is."

Her response was a sharp exhale, like a punch in the gut, the result of someone who had been praying to God to please let it not be true having her worst fears confirmed. "Oh, my God, I knew it. From the helicopter, Mike and I saw her floppy hat in the back of the car. Oh, my God. Okay, we're coming up there."

I had to hang up because Alyce and I were then approached by a slew of firemen and police officers. Some took information from me while a paramedic placed a collar around Alyce's neck.

"We need to take your daughter to the hospital to get checked out. Do you want to come with her or stay with your wife?"

I looked back at the car; Susan was still trapped inside. There was now a winch attached to the rear bumper, and they were trying to pull the car out from underneath the bus so that they could get her out. The motor whirred, the chain tightened and groaned against the weight, straining to separate the two vehicles, until either the chain snapped or the bumper gave way. I don't remember which. All I know is that the two vehicles were still fused together.

"Sir, are you going to stay here or go in the ambulance with your daughter?"

I looked into Alyce's crying eyes as she pleaded, "Stay with me, Daddy. Please." I looked back at the car again, faced with this impossible choice, and despite the guilt of leaving Susan behind, I nodded that I would.

I followed Alyce and the paramedic to the waiting ambulance. They laid her on a gurney and lifted her into the back. I stepped in through the side door and sat down next to her, and as I looked out the rear doors, I could see the team of responders still cutting away at the roof of the car, trying to extract Susan as she continued to wave her one free arm, desperately reaching for someone to please help her.

And then, as I held my daughter's hand, the door of the ambulance slammed shut and we were gone, leaving my wife behind.

We were just a few miles away from the hospital, so with the ambulance siren blaring, it took us only a couple of minutes to get there. They brought Alyce out on her gurney and wheeled her into the emergency room. I walked along by her side, holding her hand as she was whisked in.

They rolled her into the ER, and immediately a swarm of doctors and nurses descended. They cut off her new red leggings and began examining her, asking if she had hit her head, if any part of her was in more pain than another, could she move her legs, could she stand, one question after another, which Alyce answered through scared tears.

They were encouraged, initially seeing only the cuts and scrapes from the glass, but they still wanted to take X-rays. For that, they needed some additional information from me.

"How tall is she?"

"About five-one."

"How much does she weigh?"

I turned to her for the answer. "Baby, how much do you weigh?" She looked at me and shrugged, and I thought, *God, just like your mother. You're not going to tell me how much you weigh.*

I guessed, figuring it would be close enough.

And then, just as we were heading to the X-ray room, they wheeled in Susan. They parked her right on the other side of Alyce's curtained area, just a thin piece of fabric separating mother and daughter.

She was conscious and screaming over and over, "Help me! I'm dying! Help me! God, help me!" Again, the hospital personnel asked me if I wanted to stay with Alyce or Susan.

Alyce gripped my hand tighter.

"Baby, they're just going to do some X-rays, but I'm gonna go check on Mom, okay?" She nodded, realizing that she was going to be fine on her own for a couple of minutes. And she, too, wanted to know how her mother was.

Inside Susan's trauma room, there must have been about fifteen doctors and nurses crowded around her gurney. They were preparing to move her onto another examining table, but she was thrashing around so much and yelling so loudly that it made it difficult to hear anything over her wailing.

"Ma'am, we're trying to help you. What's your name?"

"Suzanne! Help me! Please!"

"Okay, Suzanne. We need you to calm down so we can help you."

Now, because they had no idea what her name really was and since she was screaming "Suzanne, help me!" they assumed her name was Suzanne. However, I could see she was in shock and was screaming for our neighbor Suzanne to help her.

Okay, let's stop here for a minute. Here's my wife of twenty-two years. We have two beautiful children and what I consider to be a good, healthy marriage. But is she screaming for *me* in the emergency room to help her? No, she's calling for our neighbor Suzanne.

There was no "Doug? Where's my husband? Please get my husband!" I was suddenly confronted with the harsh realization that if she was going to be stranded on a desert island and could bring just one person, I would totally be dumped. "See ya, sweetheart! I'm taking Suzanne. She's more capable. You understand, don't you?"

So, as the doctors and nurses continued to attend to her, asking questions like, "Suzanne, do you know where you are? Suzanne, are you allergic to anything? Suzanne, please relax so we can place you on the table," I finally turned to one of the attendants and flatly corrected them, "Her name's not Suzanne. Suzanne's our neighbor. Her name is Susan."

In the background, Susan continued to thrash around on the gurney.

I then added, "If you let me near her, I think I can help calm her down. If she sees me, I think it'll help."

"Sir, we need you to stay back while the doctors are working on her." And then a doctor turned to Susan and shouted over her hysterics, "Susan, you have to calm down! We're trying to save your life!"

They finally managed to move her from the ambulance gurney onto the emergency room table, but she was flailing around so much that she nearly fell off. When they finally got her into place, I could see that her left leg was dangling at an impossible angle off the table, and she was still struggling to get up, continually waving her left hand and screaming, "Help me! I'm dying!"

They began checking her vitals and cutting off her clothes. In a matter of seconds, she was lying naked on the table, bodies hovering over her. You know that old piece of advice, *Wear clean underwear. You never know if you're going to end up in the ER.* That one's a fallacy. The ER team couldn't give a shit whether you're in a thong or granny pants. In that moment, you are just a broken body, a piece of flesh they're simply trying to keep alive.

The next several minutes were a blur of providing insurance information to hospital personnel, statements to police officers, continued screams from the emergency room table, until they finally wheeled Alyce back from her X-rays and parked her back in her space. She, in contrast, rested quietly, listening to the screams from her mother on the other side of the curtain.

"Is that Mommy?"

"Yeah, baby."

"Is she going to be okay?"

"I think so, honey."

I actually did think so. There were no crash carts, no shouting "Clear!"—just professionals doing their jobs, moving quickly and efficiently.

For the next few minutes, I bounced back and forth between my two girls, each on an ER table and separated by just a few feet, but worlds apart. Alyce was feeling nauseated, which concerned the doctors that she might have a head injury, but she hadn't eaten anything all day, so hunger might also have been the cause. They brought her a little turkey sandwich (the one I was still holding in my hand hours later in the waiting room) and gave us the results of her leg and neck X-rays. Miraculously, there were no breaks.

Meanwhile, they began to move Susan out of the ER for X-rays of her own. As they passed, they said to me, "She's got some broken bones, an arm, a leg, but she's going to be all right. We're just going to take her for some other tests."

I remember heaving a big sigh of relief from this bit of good news. And that's when I first called Susan's mother, explaining that both she and Alyce had been in an accident, that Alyce was okay, and it looked like Susan was going to be as well. She asked if she should come out; she'd get right on a plane. I told her not to just yet. Let me hear back from the doctors first.

We hung up, and I stayed with Alyce. By that time, friends had started to arrive in the emergency waiting room, but I hadn't gone out to see them yet. I had also decided I wouldn't tell our son, Michael, anything about the accident just yet. Since it seemed like it was just going to be a few broken bones, I'd tell him when he got home from school. I didn't feel the need to interrupt his day and concern him when there was nothing he could do about it anyway.

That's when a doctor arrived and pulled me out of Alyce's area. He explained that they were working on Susan, and she was currently undergoing an angioplasty. He told me she had suffered a broken pelvis, which was causing excessive and dangerous bleeding. They had also discovered bleeding in her brain from the impact.

And now, just like Alyce, I too felt like puking.

He looked at me and solemnly declared, "Your wife is very sick."

"What does that mean?" I asked.

"Your wife is very sick," he repeated.

"I hear you, but I don't know what that means."

Again, he said, "I'm saying she is very sick."

At this point, I was getting annoyed. I asked him again, and I think he could tell that if he gave me the same answer, I was likely going to punch him in the face.

"What are you telling me? Are you telling me that it's dire?"

"If we can't control the bleeding in her pelvis, she's going to bleed out. If we *can* control it, we'll then X-ray her brain to determine how bad the bleeding is there." He would keep me informed, and then he left.

A twist to this surreal movie I was living.

I returned to Alyce's side; she had heard the entire conversation.

"Is Mommy going to be all right?" she innocently asked again. I looked at her sweet face, and though I could desperately *hope* for Susan to be okay, for the first time, I couldn't answer that she would be.

"I don't know, baby. I think we have to prepare for the worst."

That naturally got her crying again, and, next to her, I leaned over the emergency table and laid my head against my arm. I immediately flashed back to my childhood, remembering the doctor who came to our house when I was a boy and told my father that his father, my grandfather, had died. I watched from the stairs as my father took in the information. And then, after nodding to the doctor, he leaned against the doorframe with his head against his arm, much in the same way I was doing now.

I thought, *I can't believe this is happening. I really can't believe this is happening.* Random thoughts raced through my head. *Did I, in indulging in those warped fantasies of being single again, somehow create this? And if this was the end, had I been a good husband? Or would I forever feel guilty for all the unkind, unloving, petty, argumentative, impatient things I'd said and done?* I also couldn't help thinking that maybe I could have prevented it somehow. After all, it was supposed to be me driving that morning. Maybe I could have avoided the accident. But then, if not, and we were the ones who were smashed, I don't think either Alyce or I would have survived the impact in my Prius versus Susan's BMW. And, if that were the case, I don't know if Susan would have been able to get over that loss. In God's plan, if there was any plan, was this the lesser of the two evils?

I didn't know the answers to any of these questions. All I knew was that I couldn't bear the thought of her dying. But what was I supposed to do about it?

When I was ten, we had the cutest little puppy. His name was Wazoo and like a fluffy cartoon dog come to life. One day when I got home from school, my mother told me that Wazoo had run across the street and had been hit by a truck and killed. The truck driver felt terrible about it and had carried him to our side yard, where I could still find him if I wanted to say goodbye. I went outside and approached his still body. He was lying on his side and looked like he was just sleeping, his eyes closed and his mouth slightly open. There was no blood, and because he looked as cute as always,

I even put my hand on his chest to check to see if he was really dead, to see if I could feel his heart beat or his stomach rise with a breath. There was neither, so I tried something else. I tried to will him back to life, crying, "Please, Wazoo, don't be dead. Please." And when that didn't work, I tried one other thing. I prayed. "Please, God, let Wazoo be okay."

Needless to say, it didn't work for Wazoo, and eight years later, it didn't work with my dad's cancer. Twenty years after that, it didn't work when my brother contracted HIV. So here in the hospital, though I could hope and wish for Susan to be okay, I didn't turn to God for help. I was resigned to the fact that it was going to be what it was going to be.

Instead, I reluctantly called her mother back, relaying the turn of events. Again, she asked if she should get on a plane. I didn't want her to have any of her own regrets, so heartachingly, in my own acceptance of the critical nature of the situation, I told her yes.

Next, I called my mother, sister, and brother, leaving all three the same awful voicemail message, "Hey, it's me. Susan and Alyce were in a car accident. Alyce is okay, but Susan is not. I don't know what's going to happen."

I then went into the ER waiting room and saw the few friends who had already arrived: our neighbor Suzanne, her husband, Sasha, and our former neighbors, Tracy and Mike, who had called while I was at the accident scene. I told them all the same thing. If the doctors couldn't control Susan's bleeding, she wasn't going to make it.

They asked what they could do to help. I told them that the doctors were giving Alyce a little more observation time, but I expected them to release her pretty soon. Understandably, she wanted to get out of the hospital as soon as possible, so maybe someone could take her home, give her a bath to get the glass off, and get her changed? Suzanne and Sasha immediately volunteered. Then they asked about Michael.

"I haven't called him yet," I said. "Until now, it was just a couple of broken bones and I didn't think I needed to disrupt his day for that."

But now, suddenly, things were very different. I turned to Mike and Tracy. Do you think you could pick him up from school and bring him here?"

The weight of the question hung in the room. I wasn't just asking them to bring Michael to the hospital. I was asking if they could get him so that he could say goodbye to his mother.

"Of course," they said.

I moved to the other end of the room for privacy and called Michael's school. I explained to one of the administrators that his mom had been in a very bad car accident, and I needed him to call me right away. Friends were on their way to the school to pick him up.

"Could you please get him from wherever he is?" I asked the administrator. "But don't tell him what happened. Just have him call me, please."

"Of course," she responded and then added, "I hope she'll be okay."

Later, Michael told me how confused he had been about being pulled out of class. As they walked to the office, his heart was pounding, but the administrator was acting super friendly and sweet, so he didn't think he was in trouble. But if it wasn't that, then what, he wondered.

I remember having that same feeling when I was in college and got a message from my roommate that my father had called and asked that I call him back. But when my roommate handed me the slip of paper with the phone number on it, it was a number I didn't recognize. When I reached my dad, he told me he was back in the hospital and that his cancer had returned. Three months later, he was gone.

I knew what those phone calls felt like.

A few minutes later my phone rang. It was Michael.

"Hey, babe, listen. Mom was in a car accident." I paused, collecting myself. "They're working on her...but I'm not sure what's going to happen."

He knew immediately what I meant by that, and I could hear him starting to cry.

"I'm sending Mike and Tracy to pick you up and bring you here, okay?"

He managed a weak, "Okay."

"I love you."

There was nothing else to say.

Through tears, he responded, "I love you, too."

We hung up and I returned to Alyce's room. She was sitting up on the gurney. "Can I go home now, Daddy?"

"In a few minutes, yeah. Sasha and Suzanne are going to take you to their house, okay?"

She nodded.

Mike and Tracy were now on their way back to the hospital with Michael. They had discussed that they weren't going to say anything about Susan's condition, just try their best to put on a positive face. As they drove, facing forward with forced smiles, they carried on some general chitchat as silent, unseen tears flowed down their cheeks, delivering this young man they'd known since he was a baby to face the unimaginable tragedy of losing his mother.

Meanwhile, in the hospital, another doctor arrived and pulled me outside. I stood there anxiously as he told me that, thankfully, they had managed to get Susan's bleeding under control and were now going to set her pelvis before bringing her to X-ray to determine the amount of bleeding in her brain.

Though hugely relieved to hear about controlling the bleeding in her pelvis, I was also confused. Doesn't a bleeding brain trump a broken pelvis? His response brought more relief. Their feeling was that hopefully the amount of blood in her brain was minimal, and they really needed to deal with her pelvis, which was the life-threatening injury at the moment. Who was I to argue?

All of this was good. The immediate threat to her life was past. I breathed a little easier, and I could see that the doctor was more relaxed as well. It was like the "Your wife is very sick" doctor had pulled the short straw and gave me the bad news, and this one had pulled the long straw to give me the good news.

I was told that I could wait for Susan at an adjunct building devoted exclusively for intensive care patients. So after Alyce was finally released and went home with Suzanne and Sasha, I relocated to the fifth floor of that building.

I don't remember how long it was before I got a text from Mike and Tracy that they had arrived with Michael, but building security wouldn't let him upstairs. (No one under eighteen is allowed anywhere in that building except for the lobby.) Before I had a chance to respond that I would meet them downstairs, the elevator door dinged and out they came. Apparently Tracy had "persuaded" the person at the desk to let Michael up by declaring, "This boy's mother is dying and this could be his last chance to see her and say goodbye." There wasn't much arguing from the volunteer at the front desk after that.

I could see that Michael had been holding it together, but upon seeing me, he immediately let go. I took him into my arms and he cried against my shoulder, no longer a little boy in height but still a child who relied on the strength of his father and feared growing up without his mother. As he wiped his tears, I told him the promising news the doctors had given me and that I was hopeful she was going to be okay.

He nodded and asked if I had seen her yet. I told him I hadn't; the doctors were still working on her. I apologized for scaring him and bringing him here, but at the time I had called, things weren't looking very good. He understood, but also didn't really want to hang around the hospital, if that was okay. I nodded and asked Mike and Tracy if they could bring him home, which they were happy to do.

For the next few hours, I waited without knowing the full extent of Susan's injuries. I knew some were worse than others, but I also never imagined that the injury to her pelvis, which I considered a mere "break," could be as life threatening as it was. So, in truth, I really knew nothing.

Nothing...except that everything could change at any moment.

day 2: the end of the day

Susan had a very stable night last night as well as day. She was responsive today (as heavily sedated as she is), was able to squeeze my hand, opened her eyes, all good things.

The stability is obviously a good thing, as it will allow her team to perform surgery tomorrow morning. However, and without going into the details just yet, it's a very delicate surgery.

Please send some good energy for this one, and I will update again afterward with hopefully the best of news.

xxoo, d

the rest of
the enchilada

I knew that these first updates led to more questions rather than provided answers, and that there was a great deal of discomfort and anxiety in not knowing the whole picture. But in many ways, that's how I was experiencing the event; I didn't have all the information, or the information was constantly changing. In today's world, if there's something we don't know, we just Google it or text a friend for the answer. Immediate gratification. That's what we're used to, and not getting it and being forced to live in a state of information limbo can cause such intense apprehension. We're disconnected, and that disconnect can be frustrating.

This was pretty much my state of being.

I had to wait for the surgeons and neurosurgeons to give their assessments. I had to wait to hear the results from X-rays and tests. I had to wait to hear about what Susan's chances of survival were, what the next plan would be, what injury would be addressed first. There was so much information I didn't know, and some of what I *did* know I wasn't ready to share, despite the ongoing inquiries.

One of the big question marks at this point was how much damage there was from the brain injury. That first day, I had been waiting for hours when the neurologist and her team finally arrived to give me the news from Susan's brain scan. Though they previously had determined that she didn't need surgery to reduce swelling in the brain, I still didn't know how bad the bleeding was or what we could expect in terms of loss of cognitive function.

Four members of the neurological team came to find me, and together we went into a private doctor's room where they could give me the news. I brought a friend to take notes so that I could just listen and ask what I needed to ask. I was beyond anxious for the report of the scan's findings when one of the members of the neurologist's team casually began the conversation. "Hi, Mr. Segal. How's your daughter?"

As thankful as I was about Alyce's condition, I didn't want to talk about her at the moment. Still, I politely answered, "She seems to be okay, thank you."

"That's a miracle, isn't it? Is she with friends now?"

That was the end of my tolerance level for small talk. "I'm sorry. Can we just cut to the chase? What's going on with my wife?"

The main neurologist now chimed in, appreciating my apprehension. The chitchat could wait for later. "Your wife has bleeding in three areas of her brain. The good news is the spots are small and don't seem to be growing. We've been monitoring them and will continue to, but at this time, they appear to be stable."

"Do you know if there's been any damage?"

That was going to be hard to assess until she was conscious, but the doctor reaffirmed that the injury didn't require surgery and told me that whatever blood was there would eventually be absorbed back into the brain. So for the moment, another piece of good news.

I thanked the doctor and apologized to the associate for being curt. She smiled and said that she was sorry for not realizing how anxious I must have been to hear about my wife's condition. From there, I went back into the waiting room, updated friends, and we continued to wait. That was just one of the two injuries Susan had sustained that I was reluctant to publicly disclose yet.

The other one I had just learned about was that she also had a broken neck.

It's one of those injuries that makes you cringe just hearing it. And not like there's a "good" version of a broken neck, but hers was bad. She had what is called a "hangman's break," named after just that: When you're hung, you don't usually die from strangulation but rather from the broken neck. Miraculously, it hadn't killed her instantly, and from what I saw of her in the car and in the ER, she wasn't paralyzed...yet.

Her neurosurgeon arrived to give me the overview of her injury. I again took a friend with me to take notes. While trying to decipher the confusing X-rays, he took me through the specifics of the injury—where the break was, where it was in proximity to critical blood vessels, the damage to the tissue surrounding the spinal cord, and so on. He used a lot of technical jargon, and I have to confess, I followed very little of it. The only thing I could tell for sure was that this one was as severe as they come.

She had broken her C2 vertebra; it was the same injury that left Christopher Reeve paralyzed and eventually led to his death. The doctor explained how he was going to attempt to repair it—go in posteriorly (through the back) and attach a plate with screws connecting the C1 vertebra to the C3 or C4 vertebra. He admitted that it was a tricky operation, not just because it involved the spinal cord, but also because it was so close to the brain stem and those blood vessels. However, he added, it's one he's done before, and he *appeared* to be confident that it would go well. Like everything in life, I suppose, especially for neurosurgeons, appearance is key. How was he really feeling about it? That's something I will never know.

We had gotten our legal matters in order years earlier, so I had durable power of attorney to make all of Susan's health care decisions. I gave her doctor permission to do the surgery, which he wouldn't perform immediately but rather wait a day to make sure she was stable enough for the procedure. And so, once again, we would be holding our collective breath, anticipating the outcome of this delicate surgery, the one I was most terrified of.

The following morning, he advised me that nurses would keep me regularly updated with status calls about how it was going. He also told me to not be concerned if I didn't hear anything for a good period of time, as this was more than likely going to be a long and involved operation. "Try not to worry, Mr. Segal. We're going to take care of her."

I nodded my appreciation, slightly comforted by his confidence. But at the same time, I found myself managing my expectations. In high school, after taking a test, I'd tell myself I didn't do very well on it so that I wouldn't be too disappointed with the result, and if I *did* do well, then I'd be pleasantly surprised. But with something like this, I was stuck. I wanted to remain optimistic and send positive energy, yet I also needed to prepare myself for a bad outcome. In the end, hope and optimism won out, because, truly, in dark times, what else is there to hold on to?

But when my phone rang just forty-five minutes into the surgery, and it was the doctor on the other end, I couldn't help but imagine the worst.

day 3

Dear friends,
I know many of you are anxiously awaiting news on Susan's surgery that was scheduled for this morning. I just spoke to her surgeon and, unfortunately, Susan was just not stable enough for them to perform the procedure. I also know that there have been a lot of questions regarding the nature of her injuries. I'm sorry I haven't shared more with you all, but we were just trying to assess the situation more clearly, and I didn't want to provide misinformation, as the extent of her injuries is quite large.

So where to begin? I guess with what is the worst of them... which is a broken neck. I know your immediate thought is the question/concern of paralysis. The positive news is that throughout, Susan has been able to move her arms and legs and is responsive to touch, so to the best of our knowledge, other than the fracture (which is obviously no minor thing), she doesn't appear to have any other spinal injury. Again, hard to tell, but that's my optimistic belief.

As for her other injuries, the list is not small. Among them, she has upward of twelve broken ribs and some punctures in her lungs. One of her lungs is also partially collapsed. Because of this, when her surgeon attempted to roll her onto her stomach in order to perform the surgery on her neck, her oxygen levels dropped to an unstable place. So now, in lieu of the surgery, they are placing her in a "halo" to stabilize her neck and prevent any further injury.

It's an ironic choice of names for this device—halo—so angelic in what it evokes, but in actuality, it couldn't be more the opposite. What it is is a circular metal ring that is screwed directly into her skull, two screws that go into her forehead and two into the back of her skull. This piece of iron is then supported by a series of metal posts that attach to a stiff plastic vest she wears on her upper body. The result is that her head is fixed in place with zero lateral or vertical movement. And so this halo, until it's removed, will serve as a personal portable prison cell. But, I have to remember, the intent of it is not one of comfort, but to prevent the catastrophe of paralysis or worse.

Once her lungs are stronger, we'll then reassess the neck surgery. Until then, she is scheduled to have more surgery tomorrow morning in order to begin repairing the rest of her injuries, but given today's situation, I'm not sure that will be happening.

Here's the full scope of her injuries:

From the impact, she had a traumatic brain injury, which resulted in some bleeding in her brain. That has been monitored and does not appear to have worsened. We're hoping that it won't affect any of her neurological functions, but it's too early to tell for sure. However, she does respond to commands, was very vocal when she entered the trauma room (as you can imagine knowing Susan), can squeeze my hand, open her eyes briefly, etc.

As mentioned above, she broke the C2 vertebra of her neck. She has a broken scapula, which will heal on its own, her upper right arm is broken, and both forearms are broken. She has a crushed pelvis (which initially was the life-threatening injury because that ruptured blood vessels), a dislocated leg from the hip injury, a broken thigh, a broken foot, a severed Achilles tendon, and a deep laceration on her ankle.

On a more positive and significant note, she did not sustain any internal injuries, and her vitals are strong. Her beautiful face was also not damaged other than some minor burns and lacerations. All in all, miraculous, considering the impact. So there it is, and as always, your concern and love is so appreciated. But, as I've been told, and as I'm sure you can gather, this is going to be a very long haul—kind of like a triple marathon without the benefit of advance training.

Susan and I are so grateful to have such a strong support group. Her doctors have been amazing, and so, with continued luck and a lot of hard work, we'll get there.

With much love,

Doug

p.s. Here is a photo of Susan in her halo.

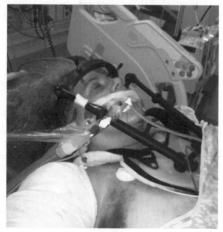

and what a village we had

From those first hours in the emergency room to the days that followed, the outpouring of love and support was phenomenal. The meal train that had been set up, asking friends to provide dinners for the next two months, filled up within minutes. A small core group continued to gather in the hospital waiting area to support me and to be there for Susan. Even though no one was allowed in her room, they still wanted to be there to send love and strength to her. I was still taking Michael to his bus in the morning before heading off to the hospital for the day. Another friend, who was a single, very hardworking mother with a child of her own, got up early and went miles out of her way to take Alyce to school, while another friend gave her a ride home. Yet another drove Susan's mother to the hospital every morning a few hours after I got there. (She had arrived that first night and spent most of her days bedside in Susan's room, watching over her little girl.) My sister had also flown in, from Boston, for much-needed moral support and to be with the kids at night, along with Susan's mother. And then there were the emails, the texts, the cards, the endless prayers...without having to utter a word, so many people were there for us.

Susan has never had a shortage of friends. She loves to engage people wherever she goes—on vacation, in our children's playgroups, the couple at the table next to us at a restaurant. Wherever we go, she gathers friends and has carried them through our lives. She jokes that "she makes the friends and I keep them," but I know that without her, my life would be far emptier. And while our "village" hails from many corners, a large part comes from our temple community.

How did we come to be part of this amazing community? If you had asked me prior to this whole event, I would have attributed it largely to something we just fell into, but again, are there really any accidents?

I was raised Jew...ish, the ellipses there to indicate my "proximity" to the religion. As a child, I went to Hebrew school and Sunday school, passed through the teen ritual of a bar mitzvah, and went to High Holy Day services with my family, but after heading off to college, I hadn't had much ongoing connection with that part of my life. As a kid, I absolutely loathed Hebrew school and Sunday school. In fact, a few years ago I was looking through some childhood memorabilia with the kids and came across my old Hebrew school report cards. They were embarrassingly awful, full of Fs, with comments detailing how I didn't apply myself or even bother showing up sometimes. Somehow the school knew that on occasion, after being dropped off for the day, my brother and I would walk in so that our mother saw us entering, but then, as soon as she drove off, turn right back around, leave, and spend the entire class time walking around town before reentering the building just in time for pickup. Yes, I was a terrific Jewish role model.

That was pretty much the extent of my Jewish identity—mainly a series of religious obligations rather than gleaning anything spiritually rewarding from the experiences.

In addition, there wasn't a whole lot of pressure from my parents to keep up any sort of practice of Judaism or to procreate within the religion. In high school and college I never dated Jewish girls; I was mostly attracted to the features of pretty WASPs and Catholics. I grew up in a fairly affluent suburb of Boston and attended private schools, so that's what I knew.

Then I met Susan, my first-ever Jewish girlfriend and the girl I would marry. And I confess, having that commonality was a nice perk. Because her parents were still alive and more connected to temple life, so was Susan. Not that her Hebrew and Sunday school experiences were so reverent. She spent most of those years making out in the coat closet, letting pimply prepubescent "nice Jewish boys" feel up her large-for-her-age boobs.

So, given our collective religious backgrounds, it was a little surprising that when it came to the accident, a big part of our supportive village was from the temple we belong to.

When we moved to Los Angeles, we weren't really looking to become members of a temple. (Neither of us had belonged to one when we lived in New York.) We were looking for a nursery school for Michael, who was two at the time. For the previous six months, he had been going to a Montessori school on Saturdays, and we figured he would continue on there for nursery school. When we found out, much to our dismay, that there wasn't room for him, we panicked. This was a crisis of biblical proportions. If you listened to some of the more hysterical parents, if our son didn't get into a good nursery school, he wouldn't be getting into a good college. After some research, we called up the nursery school at Temple Israel of Hollywood (TIOH), which also happened to be right around the corner from where we lived. We had heard really good things about the school and asked if they had any space available. Fortunately they did, and we breathed a huge sigh of relief.

Meanwhile, never in a million years would I have thought I'd be sending my kids to a Jewish day school. It's not like I had anything against it, but because religion had played such a small role in my adult life, I just hadn't considered having a strong Jewish influence in my kids' lives, especially at school. Susan was more supportive of the idea and remarked that I wouldn't even notice it. It was a nursery school, after all. How different could it be? And for the most part, it had a lot in common with a secular education... except for the occasional children's songs that would be rewritten to commemorate a Jewish holiday, like the Passover example (sung to the tune of "Old MacDonald"): "Miriam and Moses had a Seder plate, eey eye eey eye oh. And on that Seder plate they had a...shank bone! Eey eye eey eye oh."

Following nursery school, the kids entered the temple's day school, where the Jewish influence was more prevalent. Many of their classes had projects that involved the Old Testament or various Jewish holiday customs and traditions, and they also began learning Hebrew in kindergarten. And while I loved the idea of them studying a foreign language as early as kindergarten, I couldn't help wishing it was one that was a little more practical than Hebrew.

Despite all of this, I did value that the kids were getting a Jewish education and identity, and if we didn't do it here, then where? Send them to Hebrew school and Sunday school? Based on my experiences as a kid, I didn't know if I'd be able to do that. Most importantly, TIOH was a really sweet school with a great group of kids *and* parents— even though it was a little short on diversity, as expected, the most diverse kids being ones who had one parent who *wasn't* Jewish. Oooh. Not exactly a melting pot.

All in all, though, I don't regret it for a second. The kids got a great education in a wonderfully nurturing environment, and Susan and I became friends with many truly special people, who remain our dearest friends to this day. In retrospect, how lucky it was that the Montessori school didn't have space for us, and that the temple was in such close proximity to our house and had room for Michael. How fortunate we are that we "accidentally" became part of this community on which we would so heavily rely.

Things that at the time might seem like crises or aggravations can often reveal themselves later as blessings. But that perspective, unfortunately, comes only from the vantage point of looking at the events through a rearview mirror. Oftentimes, when it's happening and you're right there in it, the only thing you can see is the hell.

day 4

As much as we can try to anticipate and plan for the day ahead, sometimes life has other ideas.

That is certainly true when looking at the larger scale of events, like the day of the accident, which was supposed to go a whole lot differently than it did. But it can also be true for the smaller day-to-day moments of life. Turn the corner and an unexpected obstacle can disrupt the best-laid plans.

I'm currently feeling it on both levels, attempting to navigate an intricate route through a sea of chaos.

Once again, Susan was scheduled for surgery this morning to address some of her broken bones, but once again the team decided to postpone that surgery. The change of plan is indicative of the roller-coaster ride we're all on. We steel and prepare ourselves for events that don't come to pass and instead find that we have to deal with whatever today decides is on the menu in its place.

The decision was based strictly on precaution. Because of yesterday's respiratory problems, the team felt that having a couple of more days for her lungs to strengthen would be more beneficial than detrimental. I don't know that come Monday her condition will have improved so much more that the surgery will be possible exactly the way they would like, but the odds are better, and that's the gambling table we're playing at right now. As I'm quickly learning, it's best not to anticipate, but rather live in the moment to moment to moment.

Michael and Alyce are wonderful. Michael, while caring deeply about what is going on with his mom, also has a curiosity about what is going on medically with her. Maybe this is just his way of being able to process and deal with it, emotionally detaching somewhat like a doctor does.

Alyce, like her mom, tells it exactly like it is. Simple and straight-forward. "I hate this."

Amen to that.

day 5

Today's miracles...
 Susan squeezed my hand when I told her I loved her.
 I watched Alyce play in her soccer game.
 That's enough.

day 6

There was an old Warner Bros. cartoon about an incredible singing frog that was found by a magician. However, whenever the magician wanted the frog to perform for others so they could marvel at this unbelievable talent, the frog would simply sit there and *ribbit*. Then, of course, as soon as the crowd turned away, disbelieving and mocking the magician, the frog would come to life again, "Hello, my baby, hello, my honey, hello my ragtime gal...."

Today, Susan has been that frog. Between 3 a.m. and 6 a.m. every day, the nurses reduce Susan's pain medication so that the neuro team can do an assessment of her cognitive and extremity functions. So, naturally, when I'm in there, she's moving about, squeezing my hand, kicking her legs. And then the neuro team arrives to do the assessment, and I'm praying she'll show her stuff and get through the test quickly so that they can *please* increase her meds again! And what does Susan do? *Ribbit.*

I can't imagine the amount of focus it must take to hear anything through the pain and actually follow a command, and Susan is generally not defiant. With the extent of her injuries, I wouldn't want to move my toes either. I'd want to just lie there and hope that all these people making me confront my pain would please go away. But they won't. Not until I wiggle my damn toes.

And when she doesn't wiggle them for the doctors, I have to remind myself that this is not indicative of a bigger problem. It doesn't mean anything. Nothing means anything until I'm told it does.

Speculation leads to fear; expectation leads to disappointment.

Here's what I do know. She is moving, her eyes open but don't necessarily see, and whether she understands what's happened to her or not, I'm not sure. But I do believe she hears. A doctor friend of ours told me that she probably doesn't remember how or why she's here, so I keep telling her, over and over again. "You've been in an accident. You're in the hospital. The kids are all fine. I'm going to take care of you. You're going to get well. And you are surrounded by so much love."

Hopefully, she hears that...and tomorrow she'll wiggle those poor swollen toes.

finding
our footing

L ess than a week into this whole thing, I could already feel a shift in how I was approaching the updates. I was having a hard time confining them to simply keeping people informed about Susan's condition. There was so much else going on—specifically how it all affected my thoughts and outlook on life. Susan was fighting for her life. Me? I was trying to understand how and why we were suddenly engaged in that fight, and much of this struggle was constantly swirling around in my head.

Life at home had settled into a semblance of routine, albeit for me it was a bit of a balancing act. I generally camped out in the hospital all day, returned home for dinner, and once the kids were in bed for the night, I'd head back to the hospital. The kids were still unable to visit Susan in the hospital because of the age restrictions in the ICU building, but the truth was, they didn't need to, nor particularly want to, see their mother in the condition she was in.

Thanks to the meal train that had been set up, we had more food than we could deal with, even with Susan's mom and my sister staying with us. After a week, my sister returned home and my mother joined Susan's mom to help with the kids. Michael and Alyce continued to go to school uninterrupted, with friends and their respective schedules welcome distractions. In fact, the day of the accident, Alyce told me she still wanted to go to school the following day. I had warned her that she might wake up sore and need to stay home, but to my amazement she didn't, although she did insist on taking an alternate route to avoid being driven by the scene. I think she was also receiving a bit of celebrity attention from the accident because friends had seen images of the destroyed car and heard how she got out of the car and had the presence of mind to call me, which was amazing. If that excitement allowed her distraction from what was going on at the hospital and Susan's tenuous condition, I was happy to let her have it. I knew it would wear off quickly, and the reality of the situation would soon set in. After a day in that spotlight, it did.

Michael, on the other hand, was pretty reserved that first week, quieter than usual. I actually think that maybe he felt a little left out, a bit on the outside. After all, Susan, Alyce, and I were all receiving a lot of attention for various reasons, and he was quietly going about his business. Whenever I checked in with him, he said he was fine, so I didn't push it. Most importantly, he seemed to be able to focus on what he needed to.

In contrast to me.

The accident was all-consuming for me. While at the hospital, when I sat down to try to do work, I just couldn't focus. The only thing I found that I could write were the updates, and this was quickly becoming an indispensable cathartic release—and, most importantly, a way for me to connect and receive love and support from those who were on this journey with us.

Essentially, they kept me from being alone.

day 7

Where we last left off in our Super-Heroine serial was, "Did she wiggle her toes?" And the answer is...oh, yes. Not only did she wiggle those toes, she was flailing that right leg around, rolling her shoulders and trying to lift her body. I think instinctively she was trying to get up and get the hell out of there.

But the other big news was that when she looked at me this morning, for the first time I think she really saw me, was able to focus so much more than before. She immediately clenched her right hand around my fingers and squeezed. I again told her she'd been in a car accident, and this time her eyes went wide, a combination of alarm and realization. I told her that the kids were fine, and a sense of some calm came over her. I also told her that it wasn't her fault, and for those of you who are familiar with Susan's driving skills, you'll understand that that news also came as comfort and relief. I told her that she couldn't move her head because they were protecting her neck, but that she could still move her arms and legs, and that it was going to take some time, but she was going to get better. She just had to hang in there, fight, and let her body heal itself.

I asked her to squeeze my hand if she understood, and she did. And then I let her go back to sleep because she more than earned it. I stayed for a while longer, letting her hold my hand and sleep, which she often does when we had the privilege of doing so in our bed.

That afternoon, she was taken down to surgery to repair the injuries on her lower extremities, and six hours later she returned. They successfully repaired her broken femur fairly quickly, but her pelvis was more challenging. It was broken in the front and badly shattered in the rear along with ligament tears and other debris in the joint. Still, our doctor was pleased with how it came together. Tomorrow they plan to do an MRI on her spine, just to make sure there isn't any other damage they missed. On Wednesday, they'll do more surgery on her broken arms and right foot. And the Achilles tendon is torn, so they'll have to reattach that. I know, the list is daunting.

So here we are, seven days after the accident, if you can believe it. This morning feels like a week ago; last Tuesday, months;

and our dinner the Saturday before that, out with friends, laughing with what was, in retrospect, not a care in the world...a lifetime ago. For Susan, I hope this week becomes a faint blur. For us, it's been interminable, and of course so hard to see her this way. So keep the picture in your minds of that smiling, shining Susan. We'll get her back, but for all of us who know that smile, we also know how hard it is to go one day without it.

Until then, tomorrow morning I'll begin our "Groundhog Day" the exact same way, telling her that she was in an accident, that the kids are okay, etc., until hopefully very soon, she'll respond to me by saying, "I know, sweetheart. Do you have to keep reminding me?"

so what the hell happened?

Initially, there were many conflicting theories about how the accident occurred. Anyone seeing images of the scene couldn't comprehend how a city bus was in the curb lane after smashing head-on into a passenger car. Most assumed that the car had somehow incorrectly turned into oncoming traffic. For some covering the story on the news, it even took them a minute to realize, "Hey, wait a minute. The *car* isn't in opposing traffic...the *bus* is on the wrong side of the street!"

While it would take me over a year to start to get the real picture of what had happened (which is a whole story in itself), the true events are so random and outlandish that if I had invented them from my imagination, I don't know whether I would have written them into an action script for fear that they would have come off as too far-fetched. Truth really is stranger than fiction.

The short version is this:

Along Hollywood Boulevard, there is a series of side streets that run perpendicular to it. On one of these hilly streets, just north of Sunset, a dump truck driver parked his truck in front of the construction site where he was working. When he got out of his truck, however, he didn't place a wedge against his wheels, and while he was in the house, the truck started to slide/roll down the street. He ran out just as the driverless truck headed into traffic on Hollywood Boulevard.

As the truck drifted into traffic, a city bus (heading westbound) swerved to avoid the suddenly appearing truck, which then clipped the side of the bus. The bus driver lost control and crossed over the center divider just as Susan and Alyce were headed eastbound. Upon seeing the oncoming bus, Susan managed to turn the wheel just enough so that Alyce was spared the brunt of the impact, but the bus, still out of control, struck them head-on, pushing them back an entire block before coming to a stop in the curb lane on the wrong side of the street.

Perfect—or absolutely imperfect—timing, depending on how you look at it. One second earlier from the truck, and the bus might have been able to stop. One second earlier from the bus, and it might have been able to brake instead of swerve. One second earlier from Susan, and she might have missed the whole thing.

If only.

We can't go back in time; thus "Why?" and "If only" become futile exercises.

That said, timing really is everything.

day 9: halloween

Trick or treat?

I'd say a bit of both. A great big cruel trick put us where we are; but how many treats have followed. The biggest, that Susan is still with us eight days later. Another is Alyce, able to laugh with her girl-friends, excitedly dress up in costume and put on makeup before venturing out for one of her favorite holidays. And, finally, Michael, who continues to rise to unexpected challenges, facing them like a strong, young man.

As for me...well, I got the largest plastic pumpkin I could find, but it wasn't big enough to hold all the sweet treats of love and support given to me by others.

Susan's Halloween was spent going into surgery at around 11:30 this morning. Two surgeons worked on her arms and a third on her foot. Her main orthopedic surgeon oversaw the entire mad-science experiment, ventilators hissing, and computer monitors beeping. Six hours later, when the steam cleared and they stepped back from the table to admire their accomplishments, it was done. Titanium rods now replace bones, metal plates are screwed and bolted, tendons reattached, incisions stitched up. She was fin-ished, and she was magnificent! She's now back in her room, out like a light, and certainly seeing her returned safely from surgery was another treat for me.

So, thankfully, it was a rather happy Halloween. Michael went as a troll, Alyce as a zombie gymnast. And Susan went as herself, a combination of Superwoman and Wonder Woman—with a new, little bit of Bride of Frankenstein thrown in for good measure.

the unposted: part 1

Not to paint myself as an unreliable narrator, but oftentimes certain details were omitted from these publicly shared updates. Either they didn't pertain to Susan's condition, or in some cases, I was protecting a modicum of privacy.

One of the earliest of these unpublished accounts came on Halloween. What my entry of that day didn't include was actually how very difficult Halloween had been for Alyce. Halloween was her favorite holiday, if you can call it a holiday, and had been a mother/daughter tradition ever since she was a toddler. For months in advance, she'd plan out her costume with Susan. They'd discuss it, then change their minds, then change them again and again, until the actual day, when the decision about a costume and character was finally settled. Then came the actual dressing and makeup, all of it an intimate time for them. They'd talk about what was going on with Alyce's friends, and Susan would share stories about her childhood friends, early boyfriends, life lessons. For Alyce, Halloween was much more than wearing a costume. It had become a rite of passage, and this year she didn't have her mom to share it with.

For the entire week, we had been living not knowing

whether Susan was going to survive the accident, and though none of us wanted to face what life would be like without her, when it came time to get dressed for trick or treating, Alyce couldn't help but suddenly feel it in a very real way. I could tell she was upset about something, and when I asked her, she started to lightly cry. It wasn't until she uttered the words "I miss Mommy" that she erupted in sobs. It wasn't so much about Susan not being there for Halloween; Alyce was confronted with what *life* would be like without her. Like some holidays or sounds or smells can be, Halloween was her trigger.

Without her mom on this Halloween, Alyce experienced a different rite of passage, and like many of us do every day, she covered up her pain with makeup and a mask in order to get by.

day 10

As expected, it was a quiet day for Susan in the ICU following yesterday's surgery. Quiet, that is, except for her very swollen limbs... oh, and the ice bath she needed in order to bring her fever down... and, yeah, the hourly tube that goes down the tube that's already down her throat to suck out her chest excretions...plus waking every thirty seconds and rolling her shoulders to try to relieve the discomfort. So quiet, in fact, that by the end of the day, I had asked for a second bed to be delivered with my own Propofol drip, leaving instructions to bring me back to consciousness in two weeks when this stage would hopefully be over.

Which brings us to the little pool that I know is going on among you—you know, the one that predicts when I'm going to completely lose it, go right off the edge? For those of you who had money on today and attempted to orchestrate its success, I must confess you did an admirable job—starting with the recorded message I received at 10 p.m. last night from the orthodontist reminding of an appointment Michael had first thing this morning. But that little setback was child's play.

I do have to commend, though, whoever whispered in Alyce's ear that it would be a good idea to douse herself in glitter makeup for last night's trick or treating and then have her run into every room in the house so that I would wake up this morning to my own precious wonderland, dusted with sparkles like a sweet little fairy had puked everywhere. Clever.

But nothing compared to whoever skillfully got me to take my cell phone out of my pocket, turn off the ringer, and then hide it in some totally obscure place in the house—in this case, on the piano bench, forcing me to walk around for fifteen minutes dialing from the home phone and listening intently for a faint buzz. And special points for preying on my sanity by choosing the cell phone, knowing I would be convinced that in those frantic fifteen minutes, the hospital would be trying to reach me. Good stuff, I have to admit, but not quite enough to send me over the edge.

And then there were those of you who attempted a very different but extremely effective tack to get me to lose it: sending just the sweetest, most thoughtful texts and emails to both me and Susan, which one by one immediately caused my eyes to flood. These messages were capped by a delicious meal that was delivered to us by another angel, allowing me the grateful gift of sitting and having dinner with my children like everything was almost the way it used to be, none of us saying that it's just so very far from that.

Still, through it all, it's the end of Thursday, and my kids are still here and I'm still here and Susan's still here.

So there...we win.

day 11: friday

Shabbat shalom.

Peace and rest...in Hebrew, that's what it means.

As much as I want Susan to have both of those right now, neither is coming particularly easily. All day long she's fought a fever, tucked not so snugly under an ice blanket to cool her body, while taking a broad-spectrum antibiotic to fight whatever the infection or bacteria might be. One possibility is the IV line she's had in for a week, so they changed that out for a PICC, which is less likely to be a bacteria breeder. But then her ventilator tube could also be the culprit, or the laceration in her foot, or the pneumonia she's fighting, or myriad other causes. The team is doing its best to try to narrow it down and attack it with a more specific antibiotic. Hopefully, they'll have a better idea tomorrow.

Susan still opens her eyes far more frequently than anyone on that amount of sedation should, looking around for a moment, seemingly trying to make sense of where she is and what's happened to her. I try to tell her to rest and sleep, but no such luck. She continues to jerk her arm into the air, so it's now held in place by a light restraint and placed in a protective sleeve to prevent her from rebreaking it. And she constantly clenches and gnashes down on the bite guard that's been put in place so that she doesn't chomp through her air tube. Peace and rest...hardly.

And that's why I was conflicted about leaving her hospital bedside to go to a Shabbat dinner with the kids. It had been put on the calendar before the accident, and I know she would want me to be surrounded by friends (largely made by her) and their support and love. Upon arriving, our friend John, seeing my fragile state, said,

"Come to papa," and he took me into his arms where I collapsed in sobs against his chest.

The dinner gave me an opportunity to stop, get a little rest, and try to find some peace. It was a lovely evening, but throughout the night, it was easy to see the distress and confusion on many of our friends' faces as they, like me, grappled with and tried to understand that big unanswerable question: Why? Why Susan? Why did this have to happen? And as impossible the task of ever finding that answer is, we still try to process it, to somehow make sense of it, and hope that exploration finds us peace.

Although I remain far from convinced that this happened because I was meant to learn something from it, I still am quite aware that I *am* learning. Looking at Susan's injuries and the recovery she's facing, I think about the small steps we've already taken, and how slow and difficult those future steps are going to be.

It reminds me of a major peeve Susan has had with me in the past. It's when we're out, whether to dinner or the supermarket, and I haven't waited for her. I've walked off, leaving her a few steps behind. "Could you please wait for me?!" she'd complain. And, yes, when she called me on it, I do confess to thinking, *My God, could you possibly move any slower?!* Now, looking back on those moments, I can see that her complaint wasn't that she thought I was being rude by not waiting for her; she was hurt. She wanted me to wait for her because she simply wanted to take those steps with me, by my side, her arm linked in mine. Little steps through our life. It didn't matter where or how fast we got there, as long as we were together.

So, sweetheart, on this day and from this day forward, I am waiting. Go as slowly as you'd like, as slowly as you need, we'll take those steps, side by side, your arm linked in mine.

And that has brought me a little *Shabbat shalom.*

the unposted: part 2

I honestly don't know why people say some of the things they say.

I remember when we were having our first baby, and various people who already had children would impart their infinite wisdom on us neophytes. "Your life is never going to be the same," they'd say. Given what we were about to embark on, we were surprised when this statement didn't come from a place of enthusiasm but rather from one of doom, turning this life-changing miracle into a condemnation of something horrible and irrevocable. According to them, our marriage, as we knew it, as well as everything we did together as a couple, was suddenly going to go completely out the window. Perhaps it was a way for them to express their own frustrations or unhappiness, initiating another member into their misery-loves-company club. Whatever the reasons, Susan and I never subscribed to that glass-half-empty line of thought, and from the moments of Michael's and Alyce's births, we knew those people had been absolutely correct. Our lives were never the same. They were richer, fuller, and filled with more love than we could imagine.

That's why it was difficult when, at this stage of Susan's

injuries, some people would say to me, "Oh, your life is never going to be the same." Granted, I knew I wasn't facing the same promise and excitement that comes with raising a child, but did I really need to hear things like, "You're going to need to buy a transport van." "You'll need to ramp your entire house and equip it with handicap facilities." "You'll need to hire a caregiver." "How are you going to afford all of this?" And on and on.

It's not that I was avoiding thoughts of these possibilities; I just didn't see them as real...yet. Susan hadn't had her neck surgery, but she was still responsive, so why was she necessarily going to come out of this paralyzed? I don't credit myself with seeing the situation with a half-glass-full attitude or being intent on visualizing a positive outcome, and I'm sure that my dismissive attitude toward some of these comments was considered ignorant or naive by those who were just trying to prepare me for the reality of my future. I wasn't thinking about any of that. I was only thinking about her surviving. If she could simply live, then we'd see how the rest developed. We'd get to the learning to walk again; we'd see the extent of any brain damage; we'd tackle everything that needed to be tackled.

So yes, from the first sound of the birth of this event, the crunching metal and shattering glass, our lives would never again be the same, but there's also such a thing as "awfulizing" or assuming the worst possible outcome. And when I think about it, any and every experience in life, large or small, can forever change what's to come. It's a delicate pendulum, and I had to hold on to the belief that while it was entirely possible it would tip and land badly, it didn't necessarily have to.

day 14

I apologize for not being in touch over the past couple of days. I know that in these tenuous times, silence can be anxiety provoking. For now, Susan is doing as well as can be hoped. She's still pretty out of it, and other than an occasional squeeze of my fingers, it's hard to tell what she's really aware of. But she's still fighting. I can see it on her face, battling it out with some sedative-induced demon who has no clue who it has entered the ring with. Seeing her restlessness, the doctors doubled her sedatives in an effort to get her to sleep. Finally, worn out after twelve rounds, she succumbed and is peacefully resting, the demon back in its corner and Susan in hers until another day.

Her temperature was also still high despite the cooling blanket that covered her, so they decided to attack her fever more aggressively. A few hours into the morning, they wheeled in a large piece of equipment and hooked her up—basically what one friend coined "a personal HVAC system," with hoses hooked to material that encircles her thighs and pumps cool air, reducing her core temperature more effectively. It worked, and now she's a climate-controlled thirty-seven degrees Celsius. Tylenol left the room shamed.

I look at Susan in her bed, her hand tied to the frame so that she doesn't whack it, and just as her hand is tied, so are ours. We all want to do something, but there's so little we can do really, which is maddeningly frustrating. So we stay focused on what we *can* do: care, hope, pray, talk, laugh, share, love. If we could take all of her pain and divide it up among us, I know each of you would take a small piece. And simply knowing that *is* doing so much, more than you can ever realize.

The other news of the day included a tracheostomy, which, to my amazement and slight horror, was performed bedside. The decision to do this now was twofold: Susan's had a breathing tube in for two weeks now, and they really don't like to leave that in for more than ten days, as it can cause infection. And with her neck surgery tomorrow (for which the anxiety and anticipation is hard to mask), it's important to have an airway available if she were to go into respiratory failure during the surgery. I had to weigh the permanent scars that will likely cause, but given the options, it seemed like the best choice. So the tube was removed from down her throat, and hopefully now she can breathe a little easier.

As for me, I don't see that happening until after tomorrow's spinal surgery. Good thoughts, everyone.

the unposted: part 3

The morning of the neck surgery, a nurse approached me with some papers to sign authorizing the operation. She handed me the document, and as I read it over, I noticed a paragraph acknowledging that Cedars-Sinai is a teaching hospital and that I was giving permission for students to not only observe the operation but to participate as well.

Now, I love Cedars. They were doing an amazing job, but my understanding of this spinal surgery was that it was extremely delicate and dangerous, and between how far we'd come and the bullets we'd dodged getting to this point, I wasn't too keen on signing over this potentially life-changing or -ending surgery to a medical student. Granted, there might be some in the group who would become tomorrow's leading doctors, but they weren't there yet, at least in experience.

I asked the nurse about the clause, and she stated that it was standard because they were a teaching hospital. I responded that I understood, but that I also had some issues with it and needed to talk to someone about it. Mind you, I didn't find this easy to do. I didn't want to be perceived as difficult or confrontational or challenging their expertise, but I pushed aside those feelings and remained insistent.

A few minutes later, an intern arrived and I re-explained my issue with the clause. Naturally, because the intern was part of this teaching-hospital experience, he downplayed it and simply said that that's the way things are done there, and that it would be fine to sign the form. Sure, fine for him, but all I could imagine was that in the middle of the operation, some overeager student, who believed they were ready to take on this level of surgery, was going to ask if they could be the one to put the screw in place. And then, one tiny mistake later, Susan's paralyzed. I realized I wasn't being particularly fair or gracious in my assumptions, and much to the dismay of the intern, I asked to speak to the surgeon about it. He looked at me and said, "Really?" like, "You really want me to call one of the busiest and most prominent neurosurgeons on staff about the *authorization form?*"

I answered flatly, "Yes, please."

The staff was getting visibly nervous. Susan needed to be prepped, and I was not only holding that up, but I think they were afraid of the repercussions they were going to face over not having this form signed before now. They paged the doctor, and I waited several minutes before he finally called.

"Hi, Dr. Baron. Listen, I'm sorry to be a pain in the ass here, but they want me to sign this authorization form that gives permission for students to participate in the surgery, and I have to say, I'm just not comfortable with that."

There wasn't a second of hesitation. "Don't worry, Mr. Segal," he responded, understanding exactly my concern. "I'm the only one who's going to be touching your wife on this one."

"That's all I needed to hear," I said. "So I can cross out that clause on the authorization form?"

"If that makes you more comfortable."

"Okay, thanks, Dr. Baron."

"It's all going to be fine," he assured.

And with that, we hung up, and I exhaled, relieved. I crossed out the clause on the form and signed it, the guilt and awkwardness of making such a big deal of this firmly replaced by the feeling of satisfaction that it was going to be handled exactly the way I wanted it to be handled, leaving as little to chance as possible, while also eliminating the potential regret of looking back and wishing I had insisted on something that I hadn't.

If Susan was going to fight as hard as she could, so was I.

day 15

Until I saw her move her hands and feet myself, I couldn't breathe a sigh of relief.

But now I have, and now I can.

Susan finally went into surgery at around 7 p.m., and two and a half hours later, when the nurse called me to say that they were finishing up, the veil of anxiety and dread started to lift. I told the kids that Mom was just about done, and while we all knocked on wood, we also breathed a little easier.

The neurosurgeon called about a half hour later. He reported that the surgery had gone well, but then added news that reminded me of the danger of getting excited too quickly. He told me that when he got inside, he saw that her dura (the membrane protecting the spinal cord) was pretty badly torn, and she was very lucky to be alive (something I think we recognize all too well). He informed me that he cleaned it up, and didn't think it would present a problem in the future, but it's too early to tell for sure. It might account for some weakness on the right side, and she would have to remain in the halo for at least six weeks. He then added that because of the swelling in her limbs, he wasn't able to neurologically monitor her during the surgery, but didn't see any cause for concern that her condition worsened.

He may not have had concern, but I did. It's not like I enjoyed seeing my sweetheart in pain, but if pulling back on her sedation was going to make her move her limbs, I would be happy to see it. And later that night when they performed the assessment, boy, was I!

But this was the end of the day. Now I'll tell you how the day began:

From the moment I entered her room this morning, I could immediately sense a difference. What a change having that ventilator tube removed has made. Her eyes were open and when I took her hand and moved into her field of vision, she squeezed my hand, really looked into my eyes and smiled. She was resting more comfortably, though still active with her left hand, so much so that she completely knocked the dressing off, exposing the stitches that run up both sides of her forearm.

I went through my mantra, "You were in an accident, but you're going to be all right." I could see that she was trying to speak, struggling to force a sound out of her vocal cords. I said, "Sweetheart, you can't talk because of the tube in your throat."

And then she mouthed the words, "My babies..."

They still hadn't been allowed to visit, but I told her that Michael and Alyce were both fine, and they love her and miss her. And then she smiled again.

I went over to the wall where I had taped a photo of the four of us sitting on the beach in Cape Cod. I pulled it off and told her that Alyce had printed it out for her. She looked at it, smiled, and mouthed the word "sweet." And then with tears I couldn't hold back any longer, I told her I loved her and she mouthed back to me, "I love you, too."

Despite all the pain, the broken bones, the distress and confusion, completely in character, her first moments back came with love, joy, and a smile. Part of my worry through all this has been, How might this whole ordeal change her? But judging from her limited communication, the X-rays have been exactly right...her heart hasn't been damaged at all.

And then she began talking in a big way, mouthing things I struggled to decipher, kind of like I was deaf and had just been dropped into a foreign country without knowing the language. I really couldn't follow much of it at all and resorted to figuring out a communication system. "Okay, squeeze my hand once for yes, twice for no, understand?" She squeezed my hand twice. Did that mean she didn't understand or was just giving my hand a little extra squeeze? Ultimately, it just became exhausting, and she closed her eyes...but with a smile.

This was the "pleasant" part of the day, which quickly shifted when the medical team decided it needed to pull way back on Susan's sedative and pain medication in order to give her a neuro exam prior to the surgery. Within minutes, her joy transformed into agonizing pain. I'll spare the details of that, but suffice to say, after nearly an interminable half hour of this, they dialed her back up again and prepared to take her away. I spent the rest of the day anchored in the waiting room as 1 p.m. (her scheduled time of surgery) came and went, then 2, then 3, and so on. Hours and hours in a room weighted with worry.

Throughout the past couple of weeks, while camped out in the waiting area, I've met some other very nice people dealing with crises of their own. One such person is a man named Kevin, who has been here for his friend of thirty years whose liver has failed. Yesterday, when we were together, he told me that later that day they were going to take his friend off the ventilator to see if he could breathe on his own. If not, well, then that was going to be it. Today, Kevin's spot is conspicuously empty.

Another woman is here for her sister, who's been in the hospital for a month waiting for a liver transplant. Her sister is on a ventilator, dialysis, and some other machine that keeps her blood coursing through her veins. Tomorrow, the woman will be letting her sister go, resigned to the inevitable. And as she told me this and squeezed my hand in hers, she hoped that her sister's strength and spirit would help Susan heal. She and I, relative strangers, bonded over concern for our loved ones.

Their stories, however, are ending with the heavy heart of defeat.

And as I sit here now, on the other side of this surgery, I think back to what feels like so long ago...to this morning when I woke both Michael and Alyce with a kiss, their cheeks warm and smooth, grateful to see them smile as their eyes opened. Then later, when I arrived at the hospital and was blessed to see Susan's smile as she looked at me and mouthed the words "I love you."

It was a brutally long day, but mine ended with a heart full of hope.

day 16

First thing this morning, Susan's neurosurgeon, Dr. Baron, said to me, "Wow, she seems even stronger than before the surgery. I'm very pleased...." I had to keep myself from getting too happy, envisioning the proverbial dangling shoe. And though it didn't drop, he did go on to tell me something that definitely made me stop and again count my blessings.

I was aware that, prior to the surgery, he had decided to bring another surgeon on to join him. Dr. Baron is extremely highly regarded, and this other surgeon, his mentor, is considered one of the best spinal cord surgeons in the world. Dr. Baron told me that, in all his experience, he has never seen a fracture as bad as Susan's (without disastrous consequences), and that his mentor, in *his* twenty years of experience, has seen only two or three, reiterating again how very lucky Susan is.

When I told this to my sister, she very aptly remarked that it's incredible that someone could be so unlucky and so very lucky at the same time. Which left me thinking: *What if the surgery had gone through as planned ten days ago?* I was disappointed when it didn't happen as scheduled, mostly because I had wanted it behind me and hated the idea of it hanging over my head, looming in the future. But now as I look at it, I remember that Dr. Baron was initially planning a different surgical approach and was going to perform the surgery alone. What if Susan hadn't gone into respiratory failure, which at the time, of course, was so awful? Would Dr. Baron have been as successful going through the back of her neck versus the front, which was the original plan but wasn't the way it ultimately went. Would there have been a different outcome without the mentor there? We'll never know.

Everything happens for a reason.

Maybe...maybe not. It's one of those ideas that, even though it's impossible to empirically prove, does resonate with me, particularly in times like these. And believing that it might be true helps me stay focused on where we are right now, rather than where we were yesterday or where we're going to be tomorrow.

My conversation with Dr. Baron raised once again something I've pondered many times over the past two weeks, the whole question of What if? The first was on the morning of the accident when I was doing my work and the phone rang and rang and rang, the answering machine that lived downstairs not picking up, until finally I did and heard Alyce's tearful voice. Why, on that day, was the machine suddenly off? We never turn the machine off. But what if it had been on? I would never have heard my frantic daughter's message. I would have continued working, then taken a shower, gotten dressed. An hour would have passed without me knowing anything about the accident. I'm not sure I would have even checked the machine before leaving the house, because the messages are always for Susan. But not on that day. That day the machine was turned off, and I thankfully picked up the phone.

What if, what if, what if?

I don't know, and I'll never know. But where it leaves me now, as I face each uncertain day, is trying not to judge, or make sense of, the past, just holding on to the idea that maybe the "sense" of yesterday just hasn't revealed itself yet.

I guess that's faith—Alyce's middle name—which lives adjacent to hope and comprise a well I've returned to many times over during this ordeal. We need them both. Because even when times seem darkest, faith and hope are the bits of light we can hold on to.

day 17

Susan had an up-and-down day, which is consistent with the ride we're all on. It began with her resting pretty well, less agitated on her new medication but also fairly unresponsive. That was okay with me. I'd rather her rest and not be in pain than be present. She was still running a low fever, which the team now believes is due to pneumonia.

And then as the day progressed, so did her fever, rising past 101, 102, 103, and finally peaking above 104. She became far more restless, and as her heart rate climbed, so did mine. Finally, after hooking her back up to her personal air-conditioning unit and getting the antibiotics going, thankfully her fever broke.

Once her temperature was down, Dr. Allison, her orthopedic surgeon, who is a lovely, gentle, and caring man, arrived to check on her. He removed all of her dressings and checked to see if there was any sign of infection that might be contributing to or causing the fever. He is just one of the many good people looking after her, just as there are a lot of good people looking after me, too.

Case in point: For some strange reason, this morning the electronics in my car went screwy and the car wouldn't engage into gear. It also wouldn't turn off. In fact, it wouldn't do anything. So Michael and I sat in the garage, eight minutes away from his bus, which would be leaving in ten. I kept trying to get the car going, but as the minutes continued to tick away, it quickly became apparent that he was going to miss his bus. Great.

However, with this incredible support group we have, I quickly made a phone call and within minutes, had a friend of Susan's at the house to help Alyce get to school. I then called AAA, but before they arrived, my car finally decided to cooperate, so Michael and I headed directly to his school, having now missed his bus.

After I dropped him off, I sat in the parking lot and read a couple of morning emails and texts, drinking in their love and support before heading home. As I was driving on the congested, rush-hour freeway, I thought about those messages as well as the many, many others I have received. I thought about the sheer numbers in this support circle, which I know goes well beyond the names that are on the updates' cc list. I then started to think about the people I've encountered while in the hospital, praying for their loved ones. I see them with their families, embracing each other as they cry, offering their sympathy and condolences to me despite their own tragedies.

And tearing up (which is basically an hourly event in my life these days) over all of this compassion from so many different sources, out of my driver's side window, I looked across the congestion to a woman in the lane next to mine, also stopped in traffic. She was a complete stranger, but as our eyes met, I thought, *I wonder what pain she has in her life?* I mean, so many of us have something or know someone who has something, but is everyone as fortunate as Susan and I are to have the same support and care? How many have to face their pain with no one there to lean on, no one to provide that compassion and help? And wondering if perhaps this stranger was one of those people, as traffic started to move again, I gave her a small friendly smile, which she acknowledged, and then we drove on, never to meet again.

We see it in the face of tragedy, and lately it has been proven to me over and over again: people are good, people are kind, people are giving. Despite how cynical we might have become, it's these times that melt that cynicism away and just leave care...pure, loving care. And I'll go to sleep tonight knowing that when I open my electronic mailbox again tomorrow, there will be more messages of love and support. And they will make me swell, in my eyes and in my heart, and then hopefully, I'll remember to share that compassion with others.

Xxoo to all of you.

the unposted: part 4

I still have zero focus when it comes to work.

I tried to stay involved with the show I was in post-production on, promising to review cuts when I had time and to do notes, but I just couldn't. The production company was completely understanding, told me not to worry about it, and that they would finish it on their own. My job for Disney required just a few little rewrites, and those I was able to do. They were happy, and I didn't hear back from them about any other changes. The movie I had shot was in edit, so there wasn't much I could do there. It was the pilot I had sold that I was most worried about. Not that the other jobs weren't important, but this was a potential TV series, which could be a career changer for me.

I emailed my producer to see if there was any feedback on the draft I had submitted the morning of that fateful day. He told me that I shouldn't be thinking about that right now. "Focus on your family," he said. Which I was, but I also wanted to hear what the network's thoughts were, knowing that a loss of momentum on the project would surely kill it. I have to admit, though, I was concerned, given my mental state, how I would be able to address those notes, as all of my energy, creative and otherwise, was going into Susan's care, the kids, and into writing the updates. The entries had become a lifeline, not only for those who were following Susan's progress but an emotional one for me, given the unbelievable amount of support I was receiving.

It was around this time that I received a call from one of the rabbis at our temple. In addition to asking me how the kids and I were holding up, she wanted to inform me about a call she had received from one of the congregants. She couldn't tell me who it was—they wanted to remain anonymous—but this congregant wanted to know how I was doing from a financial standpoint as well. They were prepared to make a donation to help with our expenses if I needed it. I was left speechless.

"Wow," I said. "That is incredibly generous."

"It just speaks to how moved everyone is by what you and your family are going through."

I generally have a hard time asking for help from anybody regarding anything. Not that I haven't ever needed it, but I either feel it's an imposition, or guilty or embarrassed, or that it's admitting weakness if I can't get through whatever it is on my own. But here we were facing exorbitant medical costs (even though I was hoping our insurance would cover the majority of it); I was no longer employed and had no idea when I would be able to go back to work; we were already in a fair amount of debt, digging deeper and deeper into a home equity loan, borrowing from my sister, and racking up credit card balances. So again, why was I grappling with accepting this token of kindness? Because, ultimately, it felt like another of God's tests, that it would be exploitative of me to reap a financial bailout from the trouble I had gotten myself into, which began prior to the accident. And, if I took the offer, what cosmic consequence might I face as a repercussion? It was superstition mixed with pride mixed with guilt—the perfect Jewish cocktail.

But I have to ask myself: What good is it to have a village there to support you if you're unwilling to accept the help? And part of me felt like I was definitely playing the "It's okay, I'll just sit here in the dark" martyr. It's how I was raised. We didn't ask for help; we figured it out on our own.

So still, to this day, my reluctance to ask for help remains intact. Maybe it's because, for me and for many others, *to take* actually requires more strength than *to give*. Giving is effortless when it comes from a place of love. Taking, with a conscience, requires far more vulnerability and forces us to deal with whatever baggage we might have regarding accepting these gestures.

As for the financial offer from the rabbi, I ultimately graciously declined, but it still leaves me wondering: When someone is there to provide some much-needed light, why do we so often still choose to sit in the dark?

day 18

There's a thing that Susan does, not just with me, but with many of you as well. When I tell her I love her, she responds, "Much more" or "More." It's cute, it's endearing, but here's the thing…it's absolutely true. Her capacity to love is so great that no matter what you throw at her, she will come back at you with more.

It's how she lives; it's how she loves.

More.

Even in the state she's in, she is still able to muster that warmth and glow. Which is how it was today, a much better day than yesterday. Fever way down, she was alert and more focused. When I took her hand, she looked at me, smiled, and squeezed my hand tightly. And then she mouthed, "Cold." I got her a blanket and she mouthed, "Thank you."

And then she mouthed a whole lot of stuff that I couldn't decipher at all. But she was talking! Talking without sound, but still talking. And very connected. I told her about the accident again, about Michael's school conference today, about Alyce's speech contest last night. Some of what I said caused confusion, mostly because I think that in her mind, Michael's school conference is still a couple of weeks away, and Alyce hadn't even signed up for a speech contest before the accident.

Her warmth is hardly limited to just me. With the doctors and nurses, as battered and stitched up as she is, head locked in place within a metal dome, she still manages to give them all a smile when they come in to either check on her, shift her, poke her, adjust this tube or that line. Because that is who she is. And I know that right now if we stop and picture her in our minds, what happens? We smile. There's something about her face, her energy, her life force that brings out the same in each of us.

Today, I went to the storage facility that houses what little remains of her car to see if I could find her glasses. Miraculously I did, and among some other items, I found a headshot of hers that she kept in the back-seat pocket. I pulled it out and looked at that beautiful face, her eyes warm and blue, her smile that just makes you want to look at it again and again. I slipped the photo into my backpack so that I could tape it up in her room and the entire troupe of white-coated magicians could see the treasure who has been hidden beneath the broken bones and bruises but is finally starting to reemerge. Because they haven't really met her yet, but soon they will and soon they will know.

And, of course, at the end of the day, before I left her room tonight, I said, "I love you so much."

True to form, she mouthed back, "Much more."

day 19

"I want to go home now."

And then she'd struggle to lift her broken body from the bed.

"You can't, sweetheart. Not yet."

Then she again attempted to shift her body, unable to lift her arms because of the restraints necessary for preventing her from pulling out the feeding tube in her nose or the breathing tube in her throat.

"Why can't I just leave?"

These were some of the words I was able to decipher this morning. Susan was alert, and the staff had just recently shifted her position in the bed, but she still wasn't comfortable. After a few lip-reading attempts, I was able to understand that she wanted the pillow removed from under her arm. So I did, and she mouthed, "That's better." This relief was short-lived, however, as she began to squirm again, trying once more to get into a more comfortable position. The sad truth was that there wasn't a more comfortable position.

Then came the series of sentences I didn't understand. "Try again," I'd say, and she would, mouthing them slower and more exaggeratedly, but I still couldn't get them, which led to frustration for her, which led to frustration for me.

Each stage has its challenges: the initial trauma room and that first day, when I wondered if she was going to live or die; the subsequent surgeries and those worries; the ups and downs of fevers and respiratory issues. And here we are now, entering a different challenge—one that I'm happy to confront, mind you, but just a reminder that not only is this a marathon, but they keep changing the course and adding new obstacles every few miles.

This particular challenge: words without sound. Open to interpretation, misunderstanding, simple nonrecognition, like we suddenly speak different languages but are still desperate to communicate. She again mouthed something.

"You want me to scratch your left booby?"

Actually, that one I got. But so many others I couldn't, which left me feeling helpless, because even if I could understand a request, chances are I couldn't do anything about it. I couldn't make her more comfortable. I couldn't get her something to drink. I couldn't bring her home.

So ultimately, as happy as I was to see Susan trying to communicate, I still asked her to not talk, to just try to relax and hold my hand. Which she happily did.

I stayed for a few minutes and then slipped out of the room. Her nurse told me that that was for the better. They want her off the ventilator and, as he explained, trying to communicate only agitates her, which makes her breathing more difficult.

Unlike Susan, I understood the nurse's words only too well—like the difficulties she'll encounter from withdrawal from the pain medication, the inevitable pneumonias that will send her back to the ICU once she's been released, the hell of being trapped behind the iron bars of the halo for another six weeks. He wasn't trying to discourage or frighten me, rather the opposite, to help me steel myself for the many miles ahead. Still, the words were sobering, especially coming off of yesterday's elation of seeing Susan begin to mouth her silent words.

Then there are these words that I write, also without sound. These words that have elicited so many responses from you, stories of your own, thoughts, prayers, meaningful words shared with your loved ones, hands just being held.

And that sound I do hear...and understand beautifully.

the unposted:
part 5

I left a piece out of that post.

Realizing that Susan was going to be in the hospital for some time and would probably want to check her emails, maybe watch some Netflix or something, text me and friends, etc., I bought her an iPad. When I mentioned this to her nurse, he looked at me like I was absolutely crazy. Up until this day, this nurse had been fairly positive and upbeat, and particularly enjoyed the music I had brought in for Susan to listen to, which was full of Broadway songs, standards, Barry Manilow, ABBA, all of Susan's favorites. He would dance around the room, singing along as he checked her vitals and adjusted the ventilator...

"So when you're near me, darling can't you hear me... SOS."

"I love working in this room. Your wife has great music."

I don't know about *great*, but...

Anyway, in addition to hoping that Susan would enjoy it, I also believe in the healing power of music, so I made sure that Susan had a little iPod setup. There were times when she gestured for me to turn it off or down, but for the most part, I think it was a comfort.

Back to the iPad.

When I told the nurse I had bought one for her, I got one of those strange reactions, similar to the "Oh, your life is never going to be the same" responses that I had previously heard from certain not-so-positive people. He said, "Oh, it's gonna be a looong time before your wife uses an iPad." In addition to the comment being steeped in negativity, I felt he was really saying to me, "Oh, buddy, I'm not sure your wife's ever going to be using an iPad again."

Where's your crystal ball? I wanted to know. And even if you do base this on experience, why crush me versus saying something innocuous like, "Oh, that's nice. They can be helpful with her recovery."

I think he thought he was doing me a favor by speaking the truth, by forcing me to face reality. But when it isn't a reality, at least not yet, all this attitude really does is become a hope-dasher, and who needs that? I'm happy to face the music when it actually plays, but for now, it wasn't.

Because, just like ABBA, I was hoping for a little SOS.

day 20: november 11

I'm not sure when I started doing this, probably around the time of my first digital clock, but if I happened to look over at the time and saw that it was 11:11, I took that as a sign of good luck. And being that it was a sign of good luck, I decided that I would make an 11:11 wish and hold that wish until the time changed to 11:12, when that wish would be sealed. The "wish" over the years has basically remained the same: "health, happiness, success, and all good things for our families and loved ones." Pretty all-encompassing, but I believe when you wish, you might as well wish big.

So on 11/11, a date that comes once a year, this *entire* day should be especially lucky. This morning, as usual, I walked down the hall to Susan's room, anxious as always but trying not to speculate on what might face me. I passed by the few ICU rooms that led to hers, which I barely glanced into, just catching glimpses of family members in their chairs, solemn faces perched bedside by bodies hooked up to machinery. I heard the "toot toot toot" of ventilators as breaths were missed or tubes were bitten down on in pain, the same sounds I'd heard in Susan's room just a few days earlier.

I reach Susan's room and look inside. Her bed is empty! My heart stops as I try to process what I'm seeing. Dismissing the worst-case scenario, I think that maybe she's been taken for a test, but if she had, they would have wheeled the entire bed and hers is still there. And then it looks like the shape of her body is there, off to the side. My mind immediately races to *My God, did she manage to pull herself up and is laying half off the bed and half on the floor?!*

Then as I get closer, I realize...no, she isn't on the floor. She is actually sitting up, in a very elaborate chair next to the bed! And as soon as I walk in, her expression goes wide with anticipation, and she mouths, "Can we go home now?"

I try to explain that we can't leave, and she looks at me confused, wondering why not. I tell her that she has a lot of broken bones, and again she looks puzzled, "No, I don't." She says she wants to stand up and tries to do just that, but then quickly relaxes, realizing the effort is futile.

"Sweetheart, you should try to nap."

"I'd rather nap at home," she mouths back.

After several minutes of this back-and-forthing, her respiratory therapist enters, very pleased and with good reason. Susan has been off her ventilator for more than twenty-four hours, and, in fact, they have removed the entire machine from her room. She is breathing very well on her own, coughing in attempt to clear her chest, which is all great progress. The therapist, so encouraged, is going to recommend beginning speech therapy tomorrow, and to give us a little preview, she plugs up the air vent in Susan's trach tube and tells her to take a deep breath in and then make the sound of an "A." Susan does and out comes that "A," hoarse and phlegmy, but it is definitely an "A."

Susan's next words were "I love you," not so much to me but prompted by the therapist to say it, like when a toddler is told, "Say, 'I love you,' " and they dutifully follow. Still, it is a thrill to hear!

And then as the therapist is finishing up, Susan mouths to her, "Where do you live? We live right here in Hollywood." (My lip-reading has really stepped up its game.) I wonder how she knows we are near Hollywood when she barely realizes she is in the hospital, but what makes me really smile is that it is such quintessential Susan—making conversation, not asking for a drink or to untie her hands, but rather just pleasant socializing. And as the therapist leaves for the day, Susan mouths, "Nice to meet you."

There is no one who can make friends like Susan Segal.

And that hasn't changed one bit. So as this 11/11 transitions into 11/12, I don't know what tomorrow will bring, what setbacks encountered or steps forward made, but I do know this: One very big wish has already come true.

day 21

She's out of the ICU!

Another day without the ventilator, another day without fever, and suddenly they were moving her. Before we knew it, we were saying goodbye to our home for the past three weeks. It was both exciting and a little nerve-racking. Despite the constant trauma and tears that lived on that fifth floor, there was also a sense of comfort there...trust.

Now there would be a new room, a new team of nurses to meet, and even though I know it's one step closer to getting Susan home, it will take some adjusting...for me, anyway. For Susan, she just greeted the new nurses with a smile; they were all new friends to make, new people to win over.

I wasn't present when the speech therapist came around to do her assessment, but when I did return, Susan's new nurse came running in, genuinely excited to tell me about it. The therapist and Susan had had a whole conversation, which began with Susan giving the therapist the name of her husband. Happily, she hadn't come up with some drug-induced fantasy, which would have been recorded on the whiteboard in the space reserved for "family/contact," leaving me to embarrassingly make the correction. She told her where we live, what I did, that she spends the summer in Cape Cod. All true, and all things considered, very encouraging.

Susan will spend the next couple of days acclimating to this new environment, which hopefully will get her back on a more regular sleep cycle, and with each day, I suspect she will gain more and more clarity. I'm still not convinced she is really aware of what happened to her and where she is. But that will come, and when it does, I'm sure there will be accompanying challenges.

Until then, she's propped up in her bed, doing one of her favorite things, watching a movie. It's a romantic comedy, and I doubt she's absorbing any of it, but her glasses are on, and as she fumbles for the remote control to do God knows what, there's comfort in this familiar sight.

I sit here thinking back on the three weeks that led us to this day—the countless hours of waiting and worry, the ebb and flow of tears, the deep exhales of relief that another day has passed. Even as recent as this time has been, like a distant memory, it's behind us now. So now, with butterflies fluttering in my stomach, we enter the next chapter.

Yes, change can be scary, but it can also be really, really good.

THE
SECOND PART:
BEYOND THE ICU

don't drop our guard just yet

As excited as I was that Susan was getting out of the ICU, I was also aware that we were far from being in the clear. There was a multitude of circumstances that could be disastrous, such as blood clots, more infections, the return of pneumonia, not to mention the continued neurological impairments and potential lasting physical issues. So while I could remain optimistic, the last thing I could do was become complacent.

My limited but seemingly endless experience with all this had shown me two things: be grateful for the progress, and remember that everything could turn at any moment.

day 22

I almost turned off my phone last night.

I never used to go to bed leaving it on, but understandably, for the past three weeks, I made sure it was on, fearful that the hospital would need to reach me. Last night, though, with Susan out of the ICU, I thought, *You know, I think we're out of the woods. I could probably turn my phone off.* In the end, though, I decided to leave it on rather than tempt fate.

And sure enough, at 3:45 in the morning, it rang. I looked at the caller ID and saw it was the hospital. The head nurse apologized for calling in the middle of the night, but told me that Susan really needed to talk to me. I wasn't sure how that was going to happen, since she couldn't talk yet, so I told the nurse to tell her that I would be right there. The nurse relayed the message to Susan, who apparently mouthed the word *Perfect.*

At that hour, it was less than ten minutes before I was in her room. As soon as I reached her, I took her hand, ready for whatever was so urgent. She then looked at me and with a breathy hoarseness simply said, "I want to go home."

That was it? This crucial, middle-of-the-night need? I'm not sure what I was expecting, but I guess it was more along the lines of, "What happened to me? Where am I, and why am I in this torture prison of a head restraint?"

I told her that if I could, I'd pick her up over my shoulder and carry her on out. She smiled and said, "Okay, let's do it."

If there was any question as to whether her sense of humor had survived the accident, rest assured, it has. She asked for some soup, and then with an expression that read, *Can you believe it?* she added with a little laugh, "I'm hungry."

"Just let me get up for a minute," she requested. I again explained that she couldn't; she was too hurt. She didn't believe me. "You don't understand. I just need to walk around a little bit. My back hurts."

I denied her request.

"Then at least take off my booties. I'm so hot."

"You're not wearing booties. Your feet are wrapped up, sort of in casts." I explained that everything that's on her—these things on her feet to keep them flexed, the stiff plastic vest that runs down to her waist and is attached to the metal around her head—is necessary to help her heal.

Then she got mad, like I, in my son-of-a-bitch, controlling manner, decided that this would be the best treatment for her and had ordered all this stuff for her. "I'm sorry, sweetheart, but I can't do anything about any of this. I know it's uncomfortable, but they have to stay on. So please, try to relax and not fight them."

"Can I have some soup?"

"No, you can't have any soup. They still have to feed you through the tube in your nose."

"How about a Diet Coke?"

"No."

She thought for a moment. "A smoothie?" She smiled, her sense of humor back.

"What day is it?" she then asked.

I told her that it was Tuesday, November 13th. The accident was on October 23rd and she's been in the ICU for three weeks. She thought for a moment and said, "Wow. Crazy." I nodded.

She didn't know the half of it. I told her a little about her injuries, but I couldn't bring myself to tell her that she broke her neck, so I gave it a soft spin, "You fractured one of your vertebra, but they've fixed it. And see, you can wiggle your toes..."—she did—"...and you can move your arms, so you're not paralyzed and you're going to get all better. It's just going to take time...unfortunately, a lot of time."

She looked at me and with complete clarity offered, "I'm lucky to be here."

I formed the thought, but before the words could come out, the tears came. I finally managed, "I almost lost you."

And then she looked at me warmly and with remorse said, "I'm sorry to put you through that."

"It's okay."

"Do you still love me?" she asked.

"More than you know."

And then with another smile, "Can I have some ice cream?"

Yes, it was great Susan was hungry. What wasn't so great is that earlier in the day, she had charmed her nurse into believing that if they left her hand unrestrained, she wouldn't pull the NG tube (nasogastric intubation, or feeding tube) out of her nose. But no sooner had they turned away, then up went that left hand

and yanked that sucker out, and in doing so, removed her source of nourishment.

Taking advantage of the mishap, the team decided to give her a swallowing test to see if she could do without the feeding tube. Sadly, she didn't pass, so the tube had to go back in. Naturally, both of us were disappointed.

Even though I wouldn't be able to bring her home just yet, it would have been nice to get her some soup or ice cream.

day 23

Before the accident, if I had to define *empathy*, I'd have said it is the ability to recognize and relate to what someone else is feeling. As of late, however, I have a new understanding and appreciation of the word.

Over the past few weeks, I've received countless messages from so many of you. I've seen your faces, heard your voices, felt your embraces. And with them, while they all contain an element of compassion, they also contain pain. Your pain, my pain, and Susan's pain, all blurred together into one, all of us emotionally joined. This empathy has not been just about recognizing and relating; it's been about sharing and experiencing.

Last night, our temple organized an impromptu healing service, intended for us to try to console one another in our collective pain, to create a safe place where, together, we could express our emotional grief. The evening wasn't for just me or because of the accident, but for anyone who was experiencing a challenge in their life. I sat with my mother, who squeezed my hand throughout, hurting for Susan, hurting for herself, and hurting for me. She and I have sat together in temple on similar occasions in the past, holding hands as we comforted each other over the loss of my father, her husband, over the loss of my older brother, her firstborn son. But this time, even though she felt her own pain as well as Susan's, I could tell that mostly she felt mine. And I have to admit it was comforting to just be a son for a few minutes with a mother's hand to hold.

Overall, the evening was a perfect example of how a community's love holds the power to heal—one another as well as ourselves.

This morning began with Susan pursing her lips asking me for a kiss, to which I happily complied. Generally speaking, as soon as I walk in the room, she lights up with the same enthusiasm as a puppy whose owner has just come home.

The kiss was followed by a lot of conversation, and even though she has a trach, there's now a bit of volume in her voice, which makes her so much easier to understand. And, like always, she's interested in everything and everybody and constantly thinking about others. "Please bring the two Isabelles a little bouquet of flowers for their bat mitzvah this weekend." How she even remembered that it was this weekend, I have no idea.

Physically, she began some therapy this afternoon, stretching her stiff knees and flexing her feet. They even sat her up in the bed, her legs dangling over the side. Even though her feet have yet to touch the floor, it was a huge baby step.

And through it all, all the smiles, the conversation, the warmth of the kisses, there was also the occasional wince of pain, pain felt by her, by me, and, I know, collectively by you as well.

All of us joined together by love and empathy.

day 24

When I woke up this morning, I checked my phone and there was a text from Susan.

I was totally confused. She couldn't have sent a text. She can barely move her right hand or reach her phone on the bedside table. But nonetheless, there was a text: "Pls bring diet coke when u come." (I later found out it was dictated to the nurse.)

What is it with this Diet Coke obsession! I'm not sure what it says when someone is taken off what was basically a continuous drip of a drug more powerful and addictive than morphine and immediately craves Diet Coke. I can envision Coke's new campaign, "Diet Coke is so refreshing that coming out of a coma or three weeks in the ICU, it's the first thing you'll want to drink!" In any case, there's no Diet Coke just yet.

In fact, no food at all, probably not until next week when they perform another swallow test. In the interim, the nursing staff still hasn't learned that they need to keep Susan's hands restrained, as she's now pulled out her NG tube *four* times. After each time, it had to be reinserted, which is an excruciatingly painful ordeal involving inserting the two-foot tube up her nose and then down her throat, and then doing a chest X-ray to make sure it's in the right position. You'd think they'd get it by now!

The problem is, half of what comes out of her mouth is lucid and rational, and so she very convincingly tells the nursing staff that if they release her hands, she won't pull it out. However, if they comply, the other half, who still isn't quite clear where she is or what's happened to her, kicks in and she rips it out in an attempt to escape. So they've had to resort to tying her hands down, and now, between the restriction of the halo and her hand restraints, she naturally feels pinned down, which causes anxiety, frustration, and pure anger.

Physically, however, she is doing as well as anyone could dream, and they're even beginning to talk about moving her to a rehab facility or placing her on the rehab floor here at the hospital, but all of that is yet to be determined. Until then, I know we're in your hearts and minds. Keep us there. That, and many, many angels, Susan's spirit and drive and love for you all, and your love for her are what have gotten us this far.

And we've got many, many miles to go.

the unposted: part 6

Kids may say the darndest things, but take a grown woman with a brain injury, multiple fractures, a few weeks in the ICU, and some powerful painkillers, and she'll come out with some pretty wacky stuff. Separating the tragic circumstances from the equation, these can often be damn funny; and while I find it odd and incongruous to be laughing at anything about Susan, sometimes it's impossible not to.

To illustrate: Following the visit of a friend who had rather thin legs and was wearing black tights, Susan pulled me in for a discreet conversation. "I can't believe what she did to her legs?"

"What do you mean?" I asked.

"What would ever possess her to cut them off and replace them with those iron bars?"

"Um, she didn't, sweetheart."

"Oh, yes, she did. I saw them."

She then pointed to her halo. "I think maybe she cut them off to make this," and then added, "that was nice of her, but she really didn't have to do that."

Overall, there is a great deal of confusion regarding the halo. Because it's so foreign to her, Susan can't really grasp the concept of what it is. At one time while another friend was visiting, she pointed to it and said, "Did you see what my friend designed for me?" I wasn't sure if she was showing it off, proud of it like it was some sort of ceremonial headdress, or disliked it and was being polite because a friend had made it for her.

And then there are the hallucinations. When our friend, Geoffrey, came by to visit, he asked Susan where she'd like him to sit (because she couldn't turn her head and he wanted to be in an easy sight line for her). She motioned to a little couch that was completely empty at the time.

"Right there next to the fluffy-headed giraffe is good. They're cute, aren't they? I think there's a whole family of them here."

Then, when Geoffrey took a seat next to the giraffe, Susan once again beckoned me to come closer. I leaned in and she pointed at the fire sprinkler head on the ceiling and whispered, "Tell my mom she should take a couple of those. They're worth a lot of money...something like three hundred dollars each."

Okay, sweetheart, I'll be sure to rip a couple out of the ceiling before we go.

And for some bizarre reason, the military has played a big part in her hallucinations. She's always on some mission, on a boat or submarine traveling the oceans, always a dutiful soldier. The one thing she doesn't care for on these expeditions is what she calls "army soup," which I figure is the liquid they are pumping into her NG tube as nourishment.

Much of the time when her doctors visit, she thinks they are military personnel, and when they ask how she's doing, she gives them her assessment like it is part of an official review, her voice very formal and authoritative. "Everybody's been doing a great job. Doug's been amazing. He rescued fifty marines just this morning!"

Generally speaking, the doctors try not to smile or laugh at the off-the-wall comments. I'm sure they are accustomed to these kinds of delusions. But every once in a while they can't help themselves. Like when Susan completed her update and concluded it with, "Very good. Thank you very much. Dismissed." And then bid them good day with an official salute.

My friend, an anesthesiologist in New York, advised me that ICU psychosis is extremely common and that Susan would snap out of it in time. Causes of this syndrome have been attributed to head trauma, or the blackout effect of the ICU, or the disruption of sleep rhythms, or the drugs, or all of the above. Susan certainly has had her fair share of them all. So I'm waiting patiently for her to return to her normal self, hoping that her head injury hasn't damaged her more permanently. It's an easy fear to get lost in, especially when the delusions get dark. Fortunately, these are less common than the comical ones.

"Did you hear that so-and-so and so-and-so are splitting up?" a friend asked Susan one afternoon.

"Yes," Susan whispered, "and do you know why?"

"Why?" the friend asked.

Susan placed her forefinger about an inch away from her thumb and said, "He's got a very small penis."

I have no idea whether there was any truth to that, but this marked the period of Susan's inappropriate and thankfully brief penis-obsession stage (apparently also another common result of a brain injury). During this phase, she would come out with completely out-of-character sexual comments, as well as some fairly outrageous requests. And while nothing says sexy more than a delirious woman with broken limbs, tubes hanging out of her, a trach stuck in her throat, and head encased in a halo, I have to admit there was something titillating about it. I even thought, *Hmm, maybe a positive side effect of all this will be a spiced-up sex life.* That fantasy lasted only a second before it morphed into a neurotic nightmarish thought. *But what if she turns into some sex-obsessed nymphomaniac? I'll never be able to satisfy her, and next thing I know, she'll be seeking out anonymous sex to fulfill her insatiable desires!*

Okay, so maybe I spun it out of control, but what it reinforced in me was that I would be very glad to have Susan back exactly the way she was. I knew that with the extent of her injuries, that was highly unlikely, but I hoped we could get close. That's who I married, and who I'd happily have back again.

days 25 and 26

"I'm weary."

That's what Susan said to me as I greeted her this afternoon. And if there's anyone who deserves to feel that way, it's her. Over the last weeks, the amount of uninterrupted sleep she's had has been minimal, waking every few moments from discomfort or from being roused by a staff member to wiggle her toes, squeeze a finger, receive a breathing treatment. And then there's been her instinctive, unrelenting desire to save herself, to get up and leave and be reunited with her family, which is all part of the fight for her life. She emerged from that weeks-long battle in the ICU, and you'd think she could now take a break, relax, regroup. I certainly was feeling that way.

But it's that second wave, one we didn't see coming, that can really floor you. This is what hit me yesterday morning when I arrived. The nurses pulled me aside before I entered Susan's room to tell me she was extremely agitated. The combination of all the drugs, plus the need to restrain her hands, had culminated in a paranoid delusion. (It also didn't help that her TV was tuned to *The Bourne Identity*.)

When I got to Susan, she desperately insisted that the staff had "stapled her to the bed" and "kept her tied in the garage for the past three days while they took the children and shoved tubes down their throats."

"Sweetheart, I know you don't think so, but you've been right here in the hospital. The kids are fine; they're at home now. We have to keep your hands restrained because you keep pulling out your feeding tube."

Last night, after Susan pulled out her NG tube yet again, they weren't able to reinsert it, because after all the other attempts, they felt her throat was too swollen. That meant that it had now been more than twelve hours since she'd received any pain medication or nourishment.

No one is sure whether these delusions are reactions to too much medication or going cold turkey off it all, but since she wasn't complaining of pain, we decided not to administer any more for now. Everyone was standing by in the event that she needed something; with her NG tube out, it would have to be an opioid.

But because opioids might be the culprit of the negative reactions, they're not anyone's first choice to alleviate the pain.

As it turned out, Susan didn't require anything, and by 7 p.m., they were able to get the tube back in and get nourishment going. It's now been close to forty-eight hours, and she hasn't been given anything for pain. I look at her lying there with all her injuries and can't believe it. She's not wincing when she coughs against broken ribs or cringing when rolled onto that shattered hip. Tomorrow this may change, but as of today she has gone two full days without anything—and it boggles my mind.

Overall, the day was a busy one, with back-to-back visits from doctors, therapists, nurses, more doctors, more therapists. By the time they started pouring in, Susan had calmed a great deal, though she was still confused and kept telling me she just wanted to go home. At one point she instructed me, "Tell the kids to pack. We're leaving here in forty-five minutes," thinking that the hospital was a hotel.

Throughout the day, Susan greeted each doctor and nurse warmly. And when each completed his or her often painful individual drill, she'd squeeze their hand, smile, and say, "You're great. Thank you." And then she'd turn to me and give me a nudge, indicating with her fingers that I should give them a little something for their trouble.

Those who witnessed this were politely amused. "It's okay, Susan, we work for the hospital." After each visit, over and over again, as soon as they were out of the room, she'd hold out her arms to me, her right wrist dangling limply because of residual nerve damage, and say, "Okay, let's go."

"Where are we going?" I'd ask.

"I have to get ready for the bat mitzvah. I don't have anything to wear."

Why she's been so obsessed about this bat mitzvah, I have no idea. Since Thursday, to test her cognitive ability, I've been asking her, "What day is it today?" The answer is always the same: "Saturday."

I'd tell her, "No, it's Thursday." Or, "No, it's Friday." But in her mind, it was always Saturday, the day of the bat mitzvah.

Of all the things to remember, she's had that bat mitzvah ingrained onto her internal calendar. Yes, the persons of honor are daughters of two dear friends, but still.... So all day long yesterday, it was the same thing, holding out her arms, asking me to take her home so she could get ready. The gesture reminded me of what the kids would do when they were little and wanted to be picked up, begging for "uppy." This was Susan's uppy, and, along with seeing her spoon-fed Jell-O by the speech therapist to test her swallowing ability or seeing the nurses roll her onto her side to change the sheets, it wasn't the first time I was struck by these childlike similarities.

So when I asked her this morning, "What day is it today?" she thought and looked at me like she has all those other times and answered, "Saturday." I'm not sure if she really knew or not, but I said, "Yes, it's Saturday" and then told her that in a few minutes, I would have to get going to get to the bat mitzvah. I was prepared, ready for the outstretched arms, ready for that simple, "Okay, let's go." She looked at me, tired from the battle, tired from the tests, tired from the sleep deprivation, and one step closer to fully coming back to me. And instead of holding out her arms, ready for her uppy, she sadly said, "I don't think I'm going to be able to make it."

It wasn't defeat. It was just honest realization. All day long she finally slept. No more fighting, no more delusions, just long, long deep sleep.

And maybe tomorrow, my baby won't be so weary.

day 27

Today was much like yesterday. Susan is still confused, still delirious, and still mad as hell at me for not getting her out of there. I try to explain it rationally, but it's like trying to comfort a child mid-tantrum, frustrating and mentally painful for both of us. She was prescribed a medication to deal with these psychotic episodes, but it hasn't helped as of yet, and when I research the drug she was given, one of the side effects is the very thing the drug is prescribed for. How to treat psychosis? Prescribe a drug that "may cause changes in personality, unusual behavior, or hallucinations." We're still trying to find a balance, but there are so many possible contributors to her mental state that it's hard to pinpoint the cause and therefore difficult to find the best solution. It's probably just going to be a matter of time until we exit out of this phase, but that day won't be today.

As for her physical pain, other than some Tylenol, there's still been no medication administered. No pain medication. Really?

I can't help but again consider this enormous circle of support she has, the prayers said here and, for that matter, around the world, the empathy and energy sent. Has this collective light and love lifted Susan's pain, diffusing it and allowing it to be absorbed among us? Another unanswerable question, but by the warmth of reception I received yesterday at the now famous bat mitzvah, I cannot discount it. Assuming that I'm getting just a fraction of what is being sent to Susan, she is receiving a huge amount.

Part of this is because her need has been so "loud." Big in personality, big in love and generosity, it's no surprise that Susan's trauma is big and loud. But I can't help thinking about the quiet ones among us, the ones who only whisper their pain or, worse yet, suffer silently. From the get-go, Susan's condition has been so public; there is no cloak of secrecy about it at all. The accident was on the news all day, and family and friends were immediately notified. As I sat in services today, I thought about how many of us can't be so public about our pain, and therefore don't receive the benefit of so much love and support even when it is needed just as badly. Perhaps we have an illness that has a stigma attached to it, or a financial burden, addiction, troubled marriage? We all have something, but there isn't always the opportunity to be so loud about it.

Before the accident, I was one of the silent ones. We're advised to lean on friends, to share, to trust, to allow for the community to help, but it's not always that easy.

And so, rather than put the burden on others to come forward, to put aside their fear or pride or shame or any other reason that keeps one isolated and alone, I think it's a safe bet to just assume, not with pity or sorrow but just the understanding, that in the person next to you, there is most likely some need there. Oftentimes, the pain is just something we've learned to live with.

This morning, I was talking about how remarkable Alyce and Michael are and commenting about a child's resilience and ability to rise to what life throws at them. I don't think this resilience is limited to children, though; it's in all of us—the ability to adapt and readjust, even when it seems impossible that we could survive those "if that ever happened to me" events. Life happens...to all of us, and we persevere. We find a way to make it our new normal and to deal. And when we can lean and learn and receive love from one another, we get through.

And so I look at Susan, spending another day sleeping, still not fully aware of much yet or making any huge stride forward nor slip backward, just living another day. And it makes me think...we don't get something every day.

But at least we *get* another day.

day 28

"I can feel my brain getting clearer."

That was what she said to me tonight, and it was true. She was sounding clearer, closer to being "back," with just the occasional out-of-left-field comment.

The day didn't start out that way, though. Rather similar to yesterday, it began with a story, told with less anger but with total conviction of its veracity. I have learned to not challenge these tales, to instead just listen. As soon as I entered the room, Susan was very eager to tell me something, which she proceeded to do through her raspy trach voice.

"You're not going to believe what they did now." The *they* she was referring to is the nursing staff who, according to Susan, over the past few days, have perpetrated many heinous acts.

When I try to explain that she's confused, it's only brought wrath and mistrust toward me. So I've learned my lesson, and this time answered, "What? What did they do?"

"Well, around a half hour ago, they came in and woke me up and told me that I was in charge! I mean, I'm happy to take on more responsibility, but I don't even know the kids here. Some are thirteen and fourteen, and it's just not fair of them to ask!"

"No, it's not," I said. "They should never have asked you to do that."

"I know! It's not right!"

"Don't worry about it for a second more. I'll take care of it."

"Thank you," she said.

That was the end of it, and she relaxed with an easy sigh, now able to just enjoy me being there.

As the day progressed, so did Susan, starting with physical therapy that had her sitting on the edge of the bed for ten minutes! This was the goal and she hit it, which means the next step will be to transition into a wheelchair.

Following her physical therapy, she had speech therapy. Her voice is getting stronger, but her swallowing unfortunately is not, which means that tomorrow afternoon, she'll be getting a feeding tube put directly into her stomach. There are pros and cons to this. The pros are that she'll be able to get that NG tube out of her nose and therefore shouldn't require hand restraints, which have been a major source of her agitation. The con is that it's another tube, and our goal is to remove them rather than add them; but for the short term, it feels like the right move.

Among the various questions the speech therapist asked Susan during her session was what she did for a career. Susan answered, "I'm a singer. I love to sing...all kinds of music."

Though it's true that she loves to sing, I asked the question again. "Sweetheart, what do you do?"

This time she corrected herself and answered that she taught parenting classes and was an actress who does TV or movies or voiceovers. "Whatever someone will hire me to do," she said with a smile.

Her first answer was interesting, even if brought on by exhaustion or semi-delirium or both. The truth is, singing is a defining part of who Susan is, and music has always played a big role in both of our lives. I always joke that it's a good thing we didn't meet in high school because I would have immediately rejected her based on her record collection. But as different as our tastes in music are, we share the same love for it.

In her session with the speech therapist, when asked to speak an "A," Susan didn't just say "A," she sang it. She didn't even know she was doing it. It was just raw and instinctual.

Afterward, fairly wiped out by all the therapy, she lay there and made a little face with her mouth.

"What?" I asked her.

"I'm sorry."

"About what?"

"Putting you through all of this."

It was another part of her finally reemerging, her vulnerability laced with a little sorrow.

"It's not that it's my pleasure...but it's my pleasure," I answered.

She smiled, understanding what I meant.

Susan has always said that when it comes to marriage, she doesn't believe in acting out of "compromise." She believes you do things for each other because you love each other, and that's it. And she is true to that advice, not always happy about doing something with or for me that she doesn't want to, but doing it anyway because she loves me.

I reminded her of this and told her that *this* is one of those things.

"In sickness and in health," she said.

"Exactly."

And then she waited a beat before asking me, again that raw vulnerability poking through, "Am I going to get better?" The sweetness, the innocence, the hope, instantly broke my heart.

"Yes. You've already come so far."

She forced a little smile, and fighting sleep, her brain getting cloudy again, she looked at me one last time. "I just want to get better and sing a song again."

And then she let her eyes close and drifted off, so very tired.

I wanted to tell her, "You already have, sweetheart. It's a beautiful, sad, inspirational, and wonderful song. You just haven't heard it yet."

the unposted: part 7

It was around this time that I received the first hospital bill.

"I can't wait to see how much this is going to be," I muttered to myself.

When I opened it, it took me a minute to even process the number. This was the amount that was billed to insurance, not that I owed...yet. And the reason it took me so long to understand it was because the number didn't even fit into the little "amount billed" box. It spilled off the page to the right and was cut off, so it looked like a bizarre half-number. When I finally figured out what it was supposed to read, I just let out a laugh. $1,507,236.75.

My heart didn't sink, I didn't go to *Oh, my God, how am I ever gonna pay this off?* Instead, as I said, I laughed, because there was no way I'd even come close to being able to pay that sum. And this was only for the first few weeks or so; we weren't even close to getting released. For the time being, I wasn't going to worry about it. Fortunately, I had good coverage from the work I'd done with the animation guild. And, frankly, without that insurance, I don't know how I would have coped. It would have added yet another gigantic heap of stress onto an already barely manageable situation.

I hadn't gone back to work in all this time; I was still trying to get notes out of the network on my pilot, but the response remained, "Stay focused on the important stuff, your family. Don't worry about this right now." Rather than acting as encouragement, these words began to sound like the kiss of death, sort of like the boy or girlfriend who says, "Really, it's not about you. It's me," or "I just don't think I'm ready for a relationship right now."

This is the entertainment business, and I knew if they really cared about the project, they'd be saying things like, "Not to rush you or anything, and sorry about your wife and all, but when do you think you'll be up for tackling the notes?" Not saying anything was their way of letting the thing crash into the Bermuda Triangle of television where so many pilots just disappear. I'd keep trying, but I couldn't help feeling discouraged.

Still, the important stuff was getting better. So, like the hospital bill and many other stress inducers, I was going to put the show aside and heed the network's words, stay focused on the big stuff and try not to think about it for the moment.

If one thing had to die in this whole ordeal, let it be my show.

day 29

The best-laid plans...

Last night at midnight, they discontinued her NG tube in anticipation of putting the PEG (percutaneous endoscopic gastrostomy, or stomach-feeding tube) in today. At 5 p.m., they took her down and two hours later, she returned...*without* the PEG. The story as I heard it was that a trauma patient came in, and Susan got bumped. I certainly know what it's like to be on the other end of that, so I couldn't begrudge it too much. Priorities are priorities. And despite being disappointed, I'm just trying to hang on to that "Well, maybe things happen for a reason" philosophy.

She was complaining of neck and shoulder pain, so I rubbed her shoulders, but when she asked me to rub her neck, I dared not even touch it but rather rested my hand against it, hoping that just my touch might help. I'm not sure it did, but she did enjoy the shoulder rub, which to many of you will come as no surprise. Susan is like a needy cat or dog when it comes to massage, and honestly, I have a low tolerance for giving them.

Early in our relationship, as with most courtships, I offered to give her a massage and she eagerly accepted. As the years have passed, like other romantic gestures, the massages have dwindled, and I happily let anyone with the will and a strong hand step in. So today, when she asked, I complied and then complied again and again, switching from right to left to right. "Higher, more to the center, down, right there, good." Even as I rubbed, she had the nerve (and the delusion) to ask the nurse if they "could have a good masseuse who worked here come on by," like our "hotel" was now some luxury spa.

Following what felt like a two-day session on her shoulders, Susan's physical therapist arrived. Since yesterday went so well, today they planned to try to get her into a wheelchair. Initially, she was tired and not really feeling up to it, but knowing how important it is to get up, I pressed, and she ultimately agreed to try.

Unlike just sitting her up at the edge of the bed, this was a complicated procedure, involving disconnecting many tubes, positioning a slide board to bridge from the bed to the chair, and a lot of shifting, lifting, and sliding. But we succeeded, and she was in it!

While I felt the rush of a major accomplishment, Susan experienced the opposite, nearly crying over how hard the simple act was and growing discouraged and frustrated about her inability to do anything. I reminded her that in four sessions, she's gone from sitting at the bed for three minutes, to five minutes, to ten minutes, to now sitting in a chair. It was huge! And it was, but for Susan, in that moment, I think she realized just how long and difficult a journey this would be.

Once in the wheelchair, we cruised around the entire hospital floor, and though she initially enjoyed the change of scenery, I also think it was both scary and exhausting for her. After about fifteen minutes, she wanted to go back to her room, to the safety of her bed. I took the long route "home," and after wheeling her back we embarked on reversing the process to return her into bed. It was excruciating—painful for her and painful to watch. The ordeal took about forty-five minutes and wiped both of us out. In addition to her exhaustion, it also left her with that pain in her shoulders again.

As I rubbed her shoulders once more, she looked at me and said, "I know. This is your worst nightmare."

I leaned into her, gave her another squeeze, and replied, "No, this is nowhere near my worst nightmare."

day 30:
the night before thanksgiving

Thankful that the "How close she was to dying" wasn't any closer.

Thankful that I get to sit in a room with her even when out of frustration, anger, and disorientation she tells me to get the hell out.

Thankful she wants to go home so badly, which gives her the spirit to fight so hard.

Thankful for her mother's strength, despite seeing her daughter in so much pain.

Thankful for family and friends, who have caught so many of my tears.

Thankful for the music and laughter, which is its own medicine.

Thankful for the arms around both of us, even if miles and miles away.

Thankful for my children, who in each of them I see the very best of her.

Thankful for another day to feel.

Xxoo

days 31–33

I guess, to begin, I have to go back to Tuesday night...

I had heard two stories about why her PEG (the stomach-feeding tube) hadn't been able to be put in that night. First, there were the four traumas that bumped her in priority. The second story, however, was quite different and sounded more likely to be the real reason: When they got her into the procedure room, they realized the vest that attaches to her halo had to be modified to allow access for the feeding tube, and they weren't prepared to make that alteration in the moment. Why this hadn't been thought of in advance, I have no idea.

In any case, when I returned to her Tuesday night, I asked her what had happened and she rolled her eyes, like, *Can you believe this?* She wasn't upset, just felt like the whole thing was ridiculous. I asked her if she had been waiting in her bed down in the procedure room the entire two and a half hours? She answered yes, seemingly quite lucid about the whole thing, until she added with exactly the same casual conviction...

"And while I was down there, I had to save an octopus."

I paused, again debating how to deal with such a statement, but seeing that there was no hint of self-awareness of the absurdity of her comment, I went with it.

"You had to save an octopus?"

"Yes, and then I fixed a fish fin," she added.

"How did you fix the fish fin?"

She made a sewing motion with her good left hand.

"You sewed it?"

"Yes."

"How did you know how to do that?"

"I didn't. I just went for it."

I held back my laughter, but let a smile play across my mouth. She smiled, too, proud of what she had done. That's my girl, not content to just lay back and wait for her procedure. She jumped right in, no training, no prep, just went to work fixing that damn fish, proving that confidence is at least half the battle in doing.

In contrast to her accomplishment, I was frustrated and stepped out of the room to try to find out when the now-delayed PEG procedure was going to happen. I was told that they didn't know yet, maybe on Friday; they had to contact the makers of the halo vest. "Doesn't anyone talk to each other around here?" I asked. There was no answer.

When I left for home at the end of the day, Susan was fine, a little aggravated that the irritating tube that scraped her nasal membrane was still down her throat, but peaceful enough that I didn't worry about leaving her for the night.

All that had changed by the time I arrived the following morning.

She was not happy. She was anxious to leave, insisting we do, and not taking no for an answer. I tried to explain that it wasn't possible, but she didn't want to hear it. I left the room for just a few minutes and when I returned, apparently in a rage, she had ripped at the oxygen mask attached to her trach and once again pulled out her fucking nose tube! I couldn't believe it. We had relaxed her hand restraints because she seemed to be over pulling it out, but now we were going to pay big time for that lack of diligence.

"Sweetheart, why did you do that?! You know that's where your nourishment and medication come from. Now they're going to have to put it back in again, which you really hate."

She went off on a tear, "No. I don't care! Two thousand dollars we gave these people, and for what?! Let's go!"

There was no explaining. She didn't care about the necessity of the NG. She didn't care that her trach valve was how they were keeping her lungs clear. She just wanted to leave—now. Finally, not knowing what else to do, I played along and said, "Okay, let's go."

I got the nurse, telling them that Susan wanted to sit up at the edge of the bed. They helped me get her into position, where she struggled to get her bearings, using every bit of strength to breathe through the lightheadedness and nausea until after about ten minutes of this, she eventually relented, "Okay, I need to lay down again."

We laid her back down and she caught her breath after the huge exertion. Then, after two minutes of recovering, she said to me again, "Okay, come on, let's go."

This little game went on all morning. She even tried to negotiate with the hospital staff to get her a wheelchair so that she could go across the street, promising to return it later that day. She asked anyone and everyone who ventured into the room if she could leave. I had doctors explain it, nurses, physical therapists. And as person after person denied her request, she became more and more frustrated and angry...with me! Why wasn't I listening to her? Why wasn't I helping her? She began to cry, and I felt more and more helpless, until I finally leaned into her and lost it, the stress of the morning finally breaking me.

"I don't know what to do, sweetheart. I'm sorry. I'm trying so hard to help you, to keep you alive, but I don't know how."

It wasn't meant to be an emotional tactic, but there is something that Susan cares about more than her own needs; it's her children, and it's me. Seeing how upset I was, how helpless I felt, she immediately softened. "I know you're doing your best. It's okay."

She calmed down a little after this, but was still insisting we leave. To keep her away from her trach valve, her hands were once again restrained. "Come on, untie my hands," she pleaded.

"I can't."

"Why not?"

Why not? I wondered how to respond. She wouldn't accept that it was to keep her safe. She insisted that she wouldn't do anything, but we'd seen where that had gotten us before. Instead, I moved out of her eye line, where she couldn't turn her head, locked in the halo.

"I can't...because my hands are tied, too."

I didn't mean it figuratively. I meant it absolutely literally. I told her that I couldn't get free. I was mad and I was frustrated just like her, but I was also trying to relax, breathe, and not fight it.

Hearing this, she laid back and said supportively, "Okay, but keep working at untying them. You can do it."

I didn't like having to play these mind games with her, but I didn't know what else to do to get her through this. As the afternoon wore on, she became calmer, but since she wasn't scheduled to get the PEG put in for another two days, they were going to have to find a way to reinsert the miserable NG tube until then. I didn't know how they planned to do that, plus, she'd have to continue to be restrained, which was going to drive her crazy. Having the PEG procedure delayed was really biting us in the ass.

I met with her psychiatrist and discussed the plan for how to medicate her so that the tube could be reinserted without her flipping out. The doctor recommended a heavy cocktail of drugs, which would both keep her conscious for the tube insertion (because she needs to swallow the tube) but keep her docile enough for them to do the procedure. Okay, at least we had a plan. Whether it would work or not, we couldn't know.

The other thing I had hoped to do that afternoon was bring the kids in for a visit. In all this time, they still hadn't seen their mom. Even though this building didn't have the same visitor restrictions as the ICU, I wanted a couple of days under our belt there before bringing them, to let her voice get a little stronger, her head maybe a bit clearer about where she was. I had prepped the kids that she was a little confused and might say things that were kind of funny. Hearing all of this, on top of worrying what she looked like physically, they were apprehensive, but they also wanted to visit; they missed her. The day before, they had spoken to her on the phone, and Susan even posed for a picture that I showed them to demystify what she looked like. We were ready, and so was she, asking me to "fluff up the room a bit" in anticipation of their arrival.

But now, with the cocktail beginning at 3 p.m. and the NG tube going back in, that plan wasn't going to work. So instead of her pre-Thanksgiving treat, seeing the kids would have to wait until Thanksgiving Day. Still, it would be a nice way to share the holiday.

At 3 p.m., as scheduled, they began administering the drugs, and by 3:30 they were ready to insert the tube again. I told them I didn't want to be in the room for that, but they said it might help to keep her calm, so I reluctantly stayed. She was completely knocked out from the heavy dose of medication, but as soon as they started shoving that tube up her nose, even with enough drugs in her system to knock out a horse, she was awake and begging for them to stop. It was unbearable to watch as they held her hands down, continuing to force it in while Susan screamed bloody murder.

When it was over, through disoriented tears, she cried, "Why would you do that to someone?! Why would you shove a cat up my nose like that?! And that chicken tail?! Why would you do that, you stupid Indian lesbian bitch?!"

A complete delusional nightmare, not her finest moment, and one she will be mortified to hear about. I don't know where she got the idea that the nurse was Indian. She wasn't. Or a lesbian; I don't think so. But a bitch? Sure, after all we've been through with the horrible NG tubes, anyone who would subject her to that kind of repeated torture deserves a little bit of name calling.

It was absolutely horrific, but at last it was finally back in, and as soon as it was, the drugs took over and Susan calmed down and drifted off again. I sat and recovered as well, waiting another hour or so to make sure she was okay. As I was leaving for the day to join the kids for dinner at home, X-ray arrived to check that the tube was properly placed in her stomach before starting her food up. We had made it through. The plan had worked, well enough anyway, and we were back on track. I was really looking forward to getting that PEG tube in, removing the NG tube, and finally untying her hands.

Thanksgiving morning I got to the hospital at around 7:30 to get a little preview of her mood before going back home to get the kids. I walked down the hall, a little anxious as to which Susan I was going to find—the agitated one or the more sedate one. I've learned not to have expectations, but still, I wasn't prepared for what I did find.

As soon as I walked into her room, I saw a bunch of nurses surrounding her. I asked what was going on and one of them brought me outside and informed me they were moving her back to the ICU. Why? I wondered. She was doing so well.

Apparently, after I left, at around 7:30 p.m., she pulled out her NG tube again. How that happened, I still have no idea. I had restrained her hands *myself*. I had even made a sign and posted it over her bed that read, "Do NOT remove hand restraints! She will pull out her NG tube!" The only explanation I got from the nursing staff was, "She's really strong." My mind raced, *What, she tore through the fabric?! Ripped the metal from the bed?! Threw you aside, grabbed a scalpel and cut herself free?!* "So, we got the tube back in," the nurse continued. "Then X-ray came and took another image, and at midnight we got the go-ahead to start her feeding.

But at 3 a.m., radiology called us back to tell us that the tube hadn't been placed properly into her stomach. It had been placed into her lungs. The radiologist had been looking at the previous X-ray, one from earlier in the evening, when he ordered the feeding to begin."

"So you've been feeding her into her lungs?!"

"Yes, but she only got about ninety cc's. (Like that was going to make me feel better.) She's coughed up most of it, and we've suctioned a lot out, but her fever's spiked with a new case of pneumonia, so we're going to send her to ICU for observation, just to be safe."

Are you fucking kidding me?!

I had been mentally prepared to return to the ICU, accepting that with the scope of her injuries and the nurses' prior warnings that we might land back there. I just wasn't expecting it to be under this kind of circumstance. While they prepped her transfer, I emptied her room, once again taking down the pictures of Susan and the kids, the "Do NOT remove hand restraints!" sign, her music, her hair detangler, her glasses, her phone, dumping everything into a large bag. I had hoped that Thanksgiving would have gone a lot differently. I had hoped that the kids would have been able to make their mom smile and see that she wasn't as scary looking as they had feared. I had hoped that when I said goodbye to this room it would be because we were heading to rehab, not back to the ICU.

In the larger scope of things, all these qualified as *little* hopes and disappointments. The *big* hope was that all this wouldn't become too much of a setback...or worse. And then, trying to keep myself collected, trying to not let on how worried I was, as her bed was being pushed out of the room, she mouthed something to me that I couldn't understand. I leaned in closer. "What is it, baby?"

She mouthed it to me again, and this time I got it. "How's the fish?" she asked.

I paused and smiled. "The fish is great. You did an unbelievable job."

She smiled, satisfied, closed her eyes, and out she went.

They brought her back to the ICU building, to the same floor as before, so there was a familiarity to it. But there were also a lot of differences. When the elevator opened to the lobby, I saw the faces of the other ICU patients' family members, pale, tired, wiping tears of concern or grief from their eyes. But this wasn't my face anymore. We were beyond all that now. At least I hoped so.

I thought back to when Susan first came to the ICU; she didn't even have a name. She was known as Trauma Quebec 4912, the ID the emergency room had given her prior to getting a copy of her driver's license. Afterward, she would become an actual person, but for some reason, this took a few days. So until then, that's who she was, Trauma Quebec 4912, a really damaged victim of a car accident who was very close to dying.

Returning to the unit now, she had a name, as well as a face and body that was no longer swollen from trauma and surgery. And she had a voice, too, that allowed her to show her sparkling and funny personality. Nurses who had been with us before, though not happy to see her back in the ICU, marveled at her progress. "You look beautiful!" "You're doing so well!" "I can't believe it's you! You've come so far!"

Hearing the "toot toot toot" of the ventilators in nearby rooms and the doctors asking patients in overly loud voices to "Open your eyes" and "Move your toes" reminded me that these nurses spoke the truth. We really had come such a long way...but now we were back.

By the afternoon, Susan's fever was still high from the latest pneumonia, and she was shivering. However, afraid of raising her body temperature even higher, she was forced to lie there without a blanket, teeth chattering. Through shivers, she told me to go home and be with the kids, insisting she was going to be fine. And so, once again, I was forced to make another heart-wrenching choice between her and the children. It was torturous, but that is how I left her.

Alone and cold on Thanksgiving Day.

days 34 and 35

Well, she beat another one, and we're out of the ICU again!

Fever is gone, heart is good, lungs are clearing, and her hands are free. We lost about four days of progress, but we're now moving forward again. For all the many times I've heard "Don't dwell in the past" and "Never look back," sometimes it's hard to recognize and appreciate where you are and how far you've come until you revisit where you've been. I had forgotten that it wasn't really very long ago that Susan was Trauma Quebec 4912.

On Friday, we hoped that the PEG procedure would go through as previously planned. She was still running a fever, so that was a concern. In addition, because it was a holiday weekend, the hospital was operating on a skeleton crew, and if other traumas came in, Susan would once again be bumped. Fortunately, this wasn't the case, and she was finally able to get the tube inserted. Other than that, it was a relatively quiet day, no Black Friday shopping, just our own little post-Thanksgiving celebration; we expressed thanks for where we were despite some of the events that got us here.

She was basically back to where she had been the prior Tuesday, and still just as disoriented. She remembered that she had been in a car accident, but thought she had to go back to the ICU because she got hit in the head with a baseball at one of Michael's games. She looked at me and said, "Can you believe this? Like I needed this on top of everything." I agreed, even if for a completely different reason.

I've tried to understand her disorientation, to get a handle on when it might start to subside. The psychiatrist keeps saying things like, "Well, with a patient who has suffered a brain injury..." I finally stopped her and said, "Doctor, you keep mentioning a brain injury, but I never considered that to be a major factor for her delusions." She explained that even though the bleeding was relatively minor, it still was a brain injury and it's hard to say what the ramifications of that will be or the length of time for healing. For whatever reason, perhaps my own naïveté, I had attributed Susan's delirium and confusion to the drugs or ICU syndrome or sleep deprivation, basically everything but the possibility of brain injury.

Meanwhile, over the past two days, she's been, well, let's call it "irritable," and I've found that it's better if I spend a few hours away from her each day. That way she doesn't get frustrated that I'm not meeting her needs, and I don't get frustrated about not being able to meet her needs, like getting her a cold drink from the nonexistent refrigerator in the corner. Susan has always said that a little distance between us (like the time we have spent apart over summer vacation because she's gone Back East with the kids and I've had to work) either makes a good marriage better or a bad one worse. I consider my time away from the hospital to be the same kind of break, one that ultimately is good for both of us. It also tends to limit comments like, "If you tell me one more time why I need the NG tube, I'm gonna pull it out of my nose and wrap it around your throat!"

And while I concede that there has been a brain injury with some possible residual damage, when she says things like that, it's a pretty clear indicator that there's a lot of healthy still there.

the unposted:
part 8

In addition to having friends and family constantly checking in to see how I was holding up, they also wanted to know how the kids were. Remarkably, they both seemed to be doing pretty well. The Thanksgiving visit with their mom that didn't happen was disappointing for them both, especially since they had finally steeled themselves to seeing Susan in the halo and with all of her injuries and often confused mental state. Though of course they were missing their mom and wanted to see her, there was also a little bit of "out of sight, out of mind" going on, which I understood. They also felt guilty thinking about her in the hospital all alone.

Their lives, however, for the most part, were functioning pretty smoothly. Michael's school had been incredibly supportive, but he didn't want to be treated differently because of the accident, like being excused from taking finals or anything like that. He was just doing his best to manage things. He had his friends, and soccer season was in full swing; I made a point of trying to get away from the hospital whenever I could to watch him play.

And then there was my astonishing baby girl, who had gone to school the day after the accident and who, besides some tough times of missing her mom, also seemed to be adjusting pretty well. I would slip away from the hospital for some of her assemblies to see her address the school as student president or participate in a presentation, one time for winning the student-of-the-week award. At these seemingly simple events, looking at her up there, I'd find myself moved to tears.

Even though she appeared to be handling things remarkably well, I wondered whether there might be something being suppressed by her, something ugly that was going to emerge maybe tomorrow, maybe months down the road, maybe years. A few friends had asked me if Alyce was seeing a therapist regarding the accident. In the days and weeks following it, I know she had been called into the school counselor's office to talk and also had talked to some of Susan's friends, with whom she shared a close relationship. She told me about these conversations, casually and comfortably relaying them to me, and really seemed to be doing okay with it all—certainly as "okay" as could be expected. Still, I shared my friends' concerns that there might be some issues masked lurking below the surface and decided to pursue a therapist for her.

I found one through a psychologist friend of mine and set up an appointment. She was very nice and asked whether there were any obvious signs of trauma. Nightmares? No. Loss of appetite? No. Emotional ups and downs? No. Nothing that didn't seem appropriate given the circumstances. While it sounded to her like Alyce was doing as well as could be expected, we both agreed that it might still be a good idea to establish a relationship now, even if Alyce didn't have any obvious issues or need someone to talk to at the moment. Perhaps things would change over the next months, and if so, she'd have that trust in place. I went home and broached the idea with Alyce.

"Hey, Al, I was thinking that it might be a good idea for you to go and meet with someone to talk to about the accident."

"You mean like a therapist?"

"Yeah, you know. Just someone who you can talk to about how you're feeling."

"But Dad, I have you to talk to."

And while her sweetness broke my heart, I explained that even though she can always talk to me, there might be some things she doesn't want to talk to me about, and I don't want her to have to hold those things in.

She thought for a moment. "How long would it be for?" she considered.

"Just an hour. And you can see if you like it."

She paused again, evaluating the appointment like it was the dentist or worse. "Do I really have to?"

I could see from her face that she really didn't want to, and it didn't seem like her unwillingness was coming from a place of emotional avoidance. I pressed some more, explaining that it's like going back to the hospital for a follow-up X-ray to just check and make sure everything was still good and healthy. She still wasn't into it, and the last thing I wanted to do was impose a psychological issue onto her that she didn't actually have. Still, I wondered if, like her, I was just avoiding what should be done.

I called the doctor to relay my conversation with Alyce, and, surprisingly, she also didn't think I should push it. She said that it sounded like Alyce was processing it all in a healthy manner, and the last thing she wanted to do was stigmatize her. She suggested I leave it alone for now, and if things changed down the road to give her a call. I thanked her, and we hung up.

I can only hope that this is the right choice, as these are some of the injuries I worry about the most, the less obvious ones, the ones that might present themselves in the future. I twisted my knee badly while skiing when I was a kid, and though it healed and was fine for years, as I get older, I can feel that it's not the same as the other. It was damaged. And I fear—not just for Alyce but for all of us—that we might be carrying similar injuries inside us, ones that seem okay right now, that have healed or are on their way to healing, only to become complications later in life.

Susan and I were living in Los Angeles when the 1994 earthquake hit. It was terrifying, and to this day, whenever there's a smaller quake, those feelings of fear immediately rush back through me. When it comes time for Alyce to drive, for example, will she be able to, or is that when a subconscious, deep-rooted fear will present itself? Like the doctor, I don't want to stigmatize, but I can't help thinking about whether there are ghosts lying dormant...for her, for Michael, and for me.

Susan will clearly have scars and mobility issues from her trauma for the rest of her life. The internal scars, the ones we can't see, are equally haunting.

day 36

It's been exactly five weeks since they last saw each other, Susan and my remarkable daughter. That's when Alyce leaned over in the front seat of our mangled car and through tears kissed Susan's unconscious forehead and managed to say, "Goodbye. I love you."

Though she was there, too, Alyce never actually saw her mother in the ER that day and couldn't get out of there fast enough. Since then, I had shown her pictures of what her mom looks like in the halo. I had told her that she might say some funny things while talking to her. She was prepared but apprehensive, and a good chunk of that was about returning to the hospital.

But my daughter, like her mother, is a brave one. Walking down the hall, Alyce was a mixture of excitement and nerves, but as soon as she passed through the door and saw Susan's face light up at the sight of her, the anxiety melted away.

"Dolly!"

"Hi, Mommy."

"Look at you. You look so beautiful," Susan admired.

And she did.

She showed Susan a few of the oversize get well cards that have been made for her. Susan enjoyed them, but mostly she enjoyed just looking at Alyce.

"Have you been feeding the puppies?" Susan asked.

Alyce wasn't fazed. "We don't have any puppies, Mommy."

"Really? I didn't bring home two puppies?"

"No," and then... "but I'd like a puppy. Can we get one?"

Alyce had asked me what she should talk to Susan about, and I had told her that she could talk about anything—school, soccer, friends, whatever she wanted. I had also told her that sometimes Mom got mad at me when I couldn't let her have something to drink or couldn't let her leave the hospital.

So when it came time for Alyce to talk, the words she chose to speak were to try to help me. "Mommy, Daddy is the best and he's taking such good care of us. You have to trust him and listen to him and let him take care of you, too."

My eyes began to well; Susan just smiled at her and stayed quiet.

"And I miss you so much, and I know you want to leave the hospital, but the doctors say you can't yet, okay?"

"Okay, dolly."

Alyce didn't stay long. Just long enough to see that her mom was still there and that the hole in her throat and the contraption screwed into her head weren't as scary as she thought they might be.

And she didn't run out of the hospital as anxious to leave as she had five weeks earlier.

This time she walked out proud. And I was equally proud of her, for being such a graceful, beautiful young woman.

days 37–39

What a difference an ice chip can make. Melting ecstatically on her tongue, an uncontrollable moan escaping from her lips. I only wish I could satisfy her so well.

Three little morsels every twenty minutes, but enough to give her some tiny bit of respite. Gone is the NG tube, gone are the restraints, and now able to enjoy the sweet relief, albeit minuscule, of some moisture in her mouth. With each layer of the onion we pull back, I hope for less and less agitation, and while the ice chips are a huge step forward, they don't negate the fact that she remains confined to a hospital bed, imprisoned in the halo.

Prior to the approval of starting with the ice chips, Susan has been tortured, begging, pleading, negotiating, anything for something to drink—water, seltzer, green tea, Diet Coke. I had to refuse each plea and cope with her accusatory looks, like I was gaining some sort of sadistic pleasure from denying her this basic need.

Me, the master of her hell.

I tried for the 800th time to explain it clinically, and she responded with such a sharp bite and wit that it simultaneously pained me and made me smile.

"Thank you very much, Dr. McSegal. But I don't think you know so much, Dr. McSegal. No one has ever died from a glass of green tea or grape juice, Dr. McSegal."

This isn't the only name she's given me during her agitated

state: "Lone Ranger," "Joe Shooter," "Turkey Joe," and "Captain Rogers" being some of her other "terms of endearment" when I haven't complied with her wishes. I'm not quite sure of any of their origins or intended meanings, but they all have to do with me being a controlling son of a bitch completely set on making her life miserable.

On Tuesday, when her speech therapist arrived for another assessment and the now hotly anticipated swallow test, Susan knew the grave importance of this event. I had coached her, her doctors had coached her. "Don't cough and you'll get to start drinking." The concern is that if Susan isn't able to correctly swallow the liquids, they'll end up back in her lungs, which will then lead to another case of pneumonia.

Before beginning the assessment, I brought the therapist up to speed on Susan's condition, and I asked her if she knew about what had happened over the Thanksgiving weekend. She did. I went on to say that with the PEG tube in, the NG tube out, and Susan's hands unrestrained, we had made major strides in her agitation states, and that not being able to have any liquids was our next big issue. "It's very, very hard for her."

And then the therapist had the unbelievable audacity to say, "Well, she's being very well hydrated. She's just fixating on this."

"Fixating? Are you suggesting she's not really thirsty?!"

"I'm just saying there's a lot of confusion going on."

My blood boiled. "She has been in the hospital for over thirty days with absolutely nothing to drink, breathing through her mouth and only occasionally getting a little sponge swab that she sucks the life out of. "You don't think *you'd* be just a little thirsty if that were you?!"

I know Susan's confused. I hear it every day when she talks about what she did that morning. "I went shopping in Times Square, and then me and the girls had Chinese food in Chinatown." But she is not confused about being thirsty—just like I know how real the pain in her leg is when I lift it too high.

In any case, the therapist completed her assessment, and it broke my heart to see how hard Susan was trying, on her best behavior, following each command perfectly, giving an award-winning performance. Going in, though, I suspected she was going to fail it. I could see just from the swabs I had been giving her and

the ensuing coughs that she wasn't ready. My hopes and expectations may have been low, but hers were so high that it made it that
much harder to watch.

Still, Susan was confident she had passed, telling the therapist
that she'd "only have a little green tea or some seltzer and no crazy
meals, everything in moderation." The silence from the therapist
told me what I already knew. When the therapist left the room, I
told Susan that I needed to go talk to her. Susan stopped me before
I left, addressing me like she has never asked me for anything this
important nor ever would again...

"Please don't ruin this for me."

The decision from the therapist had already been made, but in
Susan's mind I could tell what she was thinking. Dr. McSegal was
butting in and robbing her of her salvation.

Out in the hallway, my suspicions were confirmed. I learned
that she hadn't passed the test. Though I was disappointed, I understood, but I also needed the speech therapist to do one thing for
me. I needed her to go back into the room and explain the results
and that these orders were from her, not me.

The therapist initially resisted, which made my anger flare
again. She relented, and we went back into the room, but instead
of delivering the bad news, she just started to say goodbye and told
us when she'd be back again. She wasn't going to say anything!
She wasn't even going to tell Susan that she had failed. She was
going to leave it to me to enforce the "no liquids" regime!

Susan's last words, "Please, don't ruin this for me," were still
echoing; I knew that they were more a threat than a plea. I also
knew how absolutely furious she was going to be...at *me*! I needed
to at least try to get across to her that I wasn't the one dictating the
rules. I stopped the speech therapist from leaving and said, "Please
explain to Susan what's going on."

The therapist begrudgingly gave Susan her assessment,
though in my opinion, in a half-assed way. I could tell that Susan
didn't buy it at all and was looking at me with a clenched jaw. I felt
completely let down and abandoned.

Fortunately, at that moment, her team of doctors arrived. I explained what was going on, and they interceded and explained to
Susan that, in fact, I wasn't the one who decided these things. They
had to follow the expertise of the speech therapist. However, they

also thought it would be fine to give Susan a moderate amount of ice chips, which, trumped in this case by the medical team, the speech therapist was in no position to dispute.

So we did achieve one small victory, three little ice chips every twenty minutes. Sometimes it's enough to satisfy her, and sometimes it's not. Sometimes it soothes her restless agitation, and sometimes, not even close. And that's how it's been over these last few days, predictably unpredictable for me, well, I should say for all of us...

Dr. McSegal, Captain Rogers, and the Lone Ranger.

days 40-42

Could the fog be lifting?

By today's indications, I would say so.

After receiving my usual 5:45 a.m. phone call asking where I was and what I was doing, I reminded Susan that I had to take Michael to the bus and then I would be coming to see her. She asked if I would please bring her some underwear, her sweatpants, her headset (because the phone is heavy), and a T-shirt. I told her I would, even though, other than the headset, I knew they would all just sit in a bag in her room. But at least they'd be there if she asked. And so I started the day, expecting it would be similar to the last few, which have been a mix of ups and downs.

Her physical condition has generally been progressing, but mentally she still has had bouts of agitation and anger, insisting she's allowed to drink, that she's gotten up and walked around, even showered and washed her hair. There also remains a great deal of frustration about not being able to go home.

"You get to be at home with the kids. Why can't I? It's not fair!"

She's right. "Fair" is the last thing any of this is.

I tried to explain, though much of it was met with, "I don't want to hear any more of your bullshit!"

One thing I've definitely noticed is that she's far more agitated when she doesn't do any physical therapy. Just sitting up in bed and exercising her legs can be so demanding that it takes the edge off the anger, so even when PT doesn't come in, the nurses and I now sit her up in bed ourselves. It's in these moments she usually realizes that she's just not ready to walk yet.

Meanwhile, the ice chips have happily progressed into little sips of water a couple of times a day. Whereas just days earlier, those chips were such sweet, refreshing salvation, Susan is now spoiled by the water and relents to having to *settle* for an ice chip. It doesn't stop her from trying for more.

The other day her friend Deb came to visit, and Susan, when she thought I wasn't looking or paying attention, motioned for Deb to come closer and lean in. Deb could immediately tell there was something shifty about her demeanor and wondered what she could possibly want. After all, every painkiller imaginable was available to her. All she had to do was ask.

Meanwhile, Deb bent down and Susan whispered, "I need you to get something for me."

"What is it?" Deb asked, panicking over what kind of illicit contraband her dear friend was going to be counting on her to provide.

"I need you to sneak me in a couple of Diet Cokes."

Oh, my God, will this never end?!

In addition to the battle over the liquids, I keep waiting for the confinement of the halo to set her off. Occasionally, she'll complain about its weight, the heaviness on her chest, and, of course, the pins in her head, but overall she's been tolerating it fairly well. I'm hesitant to even write this, though, for the same reason I don't talk about how good the traffic is prior to arriving at my destination: the jinx factor. We just need to make it through the next three and half weeks, when the CT scan will show us if her neck has fused enough for the halo to be removed.

One of the definite highlights of the past few days was finally being able to bring Michael to see her. Between the Thanksgiving screwup, the subsequent trip to the ICU, and his very busy schedule, we just hadn't been able to make that happen. But after his soccer game on Friday night, we decided to drop in on our way home, and though she wasn't particularly pleased with me for the usual unjustified reasons, she loved seeing our boy. Even as annoyed with me as she was, watching her as she took him in, seeing her proud smile as he calmed her agitation, it was easy to see exactly what she was thinking: "We did good with him." She was right about that.

On Sunday, I brought both kids back for a visit, and sitting up in her cardiac chair, Susan anxiously awaited stories from them both, gobbling up every morsel of their deliciousness until she got too tired. Then they watched with fascination as she was transferred from the elaborate contraption of a chair back to the bed.

This morning, walking toward her room, I was once again nervous about what I would face. I found her to be much clearer than on previous mornings. As we talked, I could sense she had a better understanding of where she was, that there wasn't a second level to her hospital room where the rest of us lived. She also seemed to more closely comprehend the amount of time she's been there, even accepting that some of the things that she's insisted were real didn't in fact happen.

"We don't really have a yacht submarine?"

"No, sweetheart, I think you just dreamt that."

Along with the fifty marines I saved by driving them from Boca Raton to Los Angeles, and the monkeys running wild at one of the nearby private schools, and the Thanksgiving dinner she went to where she was forced to sit in the corner the entire time. (I didn't bring up the fish she saved. She's been a hero in so many ways, I didn't want to take that one away just yet.)

"Wow," she said. "That's crazy."

I nodded. And then she wanted to know about the accident and what exactly had happened. I told her some of it, about the truck whose brakes didn't hold and about the bus that swerved and smashed into her. And I also told her about how she managed to turn the wheel just enough to protect Alyce.

"I saved my baby doll."

I nodded that she had, and her eyes welled, proud of her actions but also understanding how close we were to the unimaginable tragedy of losing our daughter.

By the end of the day, there were many more milestones. She had a good session with PT; she was able to successfully swallow with the speech therapist and will be starting on soft food tomorrow, bringing her closer and closer to that first and hotly anticipated sip of Diet Coke. And she had her trach removed! I also believe that very shortly, the PICC line will be coming out as well as her Foley catheter (to drain urine), leaving my girl with a great deal of physical rehab ahead but, hopefully, the major medical concerns behind us.

Still, as I write these words, I can't help but think about traffic, nagged that I'm speaking too soon. It's that thing about hope, such a close relative to expectation, that can so easily lead to disappointment.

But as another friend wrote to me...what's the alternative?

days 43–45

Susan's team of doctors entered her room like every other day, and in those too-loud voices said, "Good morning, Susan. How are you today?"

Susan looked at them and, with a scrunched-up face, answered..."I got hit by a bus."

She wasn't being sarcastic or snarky. It was the simple fact that she now clearly understood. And because they're doctors and they're not supposed to, but because she's Susan, they couldn't help but smile a little.

"Yes, you did. And do you know about your injuries?"

"Yeah, I got smashed."

They went into a little more detail with her, and for the first time, they were also able have a conversation with her that she could both understand and retain. They discussed where she was medically, how they hoped that in a week's time they could remove her catheter, that they were pleased with her swallowing, and that now the focus was on her rehabilitation.

Rehab. The flip side of Susan's newfound clarity is the harsh realization of the enormous task that lies ahead, and the fear and apprehension that go along with it—not to mention, the pain. Earlier, the physical therapist had worked on her so hard that, in agony afterward, Susan feared that her hip was broken again. For me, I was comforted by the fact that she was actually able to *feel* pain. Her brain was really working again. (Plus, I had the comfort of knowing that they would be taking X-rays later in the day in case they really did mess something up.)

When the doctors left the room, feeling overwhelmed by it all, she said to me, "I'm scared I won't be able to do it."

She's heard from so many people that it's going to be a long road and to be patient. "Don't measure your progress in days, but in weeks," they've said. She understands that intellectually but, emotionally, looks at herself lying immobile in bed, exhausted by the mere task of sitting up, mentally ticking off her multiple injuries, and can't help but feel daunted and dejected.

"Maybe it would have been better if it had just offed me."

This wasn't said to elicit sympathy or for me to bolster her ego. It was the simple truth of what she was feeling. The thing is, as heartbreaking as it was to hear her say that, I wasn't discouraged. In fact, I felt the opposite. To have her back with me now being so rational was completely affirming. And I had the benefit of witnessing what she wasn't yet aware of.

"Sweetheart, you have to understand something. I've watched you for the past five weeks battling and fighting a fight that many didn't expect you to win. It was pure survival instinct, something you did unconsciously. It was really hard, but you did it. So now you're going to have to *choose* to fight that hard through this next part, and because it's not just instinct, it's going to feel harder. But I don't doubt for a second that you have it in you. Because I've seen it in you."

She smiled and said I was sweet. But I wasn't being sweet. I was being as truthful about this as she was about her fear. She had lost five weeks of her life; however, during that time, my conviction about her strength and determination was just one of the many things I've gained.

I feel good about where we are and where we're heading. That's not to say that I think for a second it's going to be easy. I felt the same when we left the ICU and entered into this chapter. I was thrilled to have the life-and-death anxiety behind me, but I never imagined the difficulty dealing with the delusions, the anger, and the helplessness I faced as she was coming out of it. I suspect as we move into this next chapter, there will be the same kind of unanticipated, really difficult challenges on the road ahead.

But it's a road that from the beginning I had hoped we'd have the luck and privilege of traveling.

the unposted: part 9

I finally heard back from the network on my pilot...

They weren't into it.

I can't say I was surprised. Too much time had gone by, and pilots had already been ordered into production while I hadn't even received any notes on mine. While not surprised, I was still disappointed. This was a big opportunity, but even more than the career opportunity, there was the financial opportunity, especially in light of not having had any income for some time and bills continuing to flood in.

Fortunately, my insurance was covering the bulk of the medical, but there were still co-pays, bills from out-of-network doctors I never even knew treated Susan, ambulance bills, ER bills, mortgage and credit card payments, and on and on. Christmas break was coming soon, and I didn't want the kids to have to hang out at home doing nothing, so I booked them a trip Back East to Vermont to stay with my mother and sister. At least they'd have some semblance of a holiday and be able to get away from all of this for a little bit. Of course, that was an expense, too. The takeaway from all of this was that I really needed to think about going back to work soon. I just didn't see it as a reality, though, for at least another month. What I was doing now was more than a full-time job.

In ways, my work as a producer had prepared me fairly well for this new "job" I had taken on, or rather, plunged into. In my career, I've had to manage large staffs, keeping informed and on top of multiple departments, regardless of their diverse functions. The hours were long and the stakes were high, as was the pressure.

Here I was in a very similar environment, yet with stakes that made production on a movie or TV show seem absolutely trivial in comparison. Also like when working in production, you're not thinking about the energy expended while you're in the weeds of it. You just feel it at the end of the day when you finally stop.

In this new world, I was learning that, as good as some of the doctors and nurses were, they were also human and fallible. And just as I had heard it so many times before the accident, it is true that you have to advocate, advocate, advocate. It's critical to ask, to question, to double-check, to be a pain in the ass, to be meticulous, to be on top of absolutely everything. It's their job, but it's our lives.

So while my other show didn't go, this was the series I was in production on now, and it had every element of a great drama—a roller-coaster story, humor, heartbreak...and a truly remarkable lead.

day 46

I held the spoon in front of her mouth.

"What is this?" she asked.

"Pureed sausages."

She tried a bite. "Okay, weird...and kind of disgusting."

They were. "Want to give the pureed French toast a try?"

Welcome to breakfast. But it was food! Delivered from a spoon rather than through a tube. She still can't have thin liquids, so all the fruit juices are thickened, even the water, giving them the consistency of unset gelatin. We'll definitely have to find some foods that are tolerable for human consumption, because even if she *could* swallow the grainy pureed chicken with vegetables, I don't blame her for not wanting to. I looked down the menu at future meal choices: "Pureed pot roast with carrots, pureed turkey, pureed chicken enchiladas, pureed lasagna." Even after not eating for six weeks, it's hard to get excited by any of the choices.

I gave her a spoonful of diced pears.

"Oh, my God, I'm chewing. It feels so weird to be chewing."

I watched with glee, the same feeling I had when feeding my babies for the first time, unconsciously chewing along, desperately worried she might choke at any second from too big of a bite. But she was eating! Another big milestone and closer to getting one more tube removed from her body.

Her spirits have generally been good, still daunted by the physical therapy ahead of her but gearing up for the long, hard road, and intellectually embracing it. I hear her saying to the doctors again and again..."I want to do it for my kids and my husband. I want to get home, but I'm just scared."

The response is always the same: "You're gonna get there. You're strong. It'll take time, so be patient."

Strength is absolutely Susan. Patience, not so much.

She nodded, wanting to believe it, but I could see the doubt in her eyes. Later in the day, when she heard that her physical therapist was going to try to stand her up, her anxiety mounted.

"We'll just try, sweetheart. That's all we can do. Maybe you'll be able to and maybe you won't, but either way, don't worry. We'll just take it one day at time."

A couple of hours passed before the team finally arrived, first wheeling in an elaborate walker-type contraption and then disappearing again, leaving the walker just sitting there as a foreboding hint of what was to come. Fortunately, because she was locked in the halo, it wasn't something that stared her in the face. But it did to me.

Eventually, three therapists arrived with the nurse and prepared for the standing attempt. It took a while. The "walker" was adjusted and tested for strength, her feeding tube was flushed and capped, the bed was lowered, her walking boot was strapped on, strategies were formed, then dismissed and reformed again. Susan became more and more nervous. "What are we going to do?" she asked.

"We're just going to try to stand up, okay?"

"Okay. I was worried you were going to make me run on the treadmill or something."

They smiled. "No, we're just going to stand."

Just going to stand, I thought.

It was time to try.

They sat Susan up on the edge of the bed and she looked great, sitting straighter, breathing easier, not dizzy or nauseated, just terrified. And then she started to cry.

"Are you okay?" the therapist asked.

Through tears she said, "I just want to do a good job for you."

"Don't worry about us. You just do a good job for you."

She swallowed back her tears and readied herself. They brought the walker closer and locked the wheels.

"Are you ready to try?"

"I don't know. I think so. I'm scared."

She sat there, looking so vulnerable. They positioned themselves, but then instead of proceeding, they stepped back and quietly conferred among themselves some more. And then they pulled the walker away from the bed, putting it aside.

Susan asked, "What's going on? We're not going to do it?"

"We think it'll be better if we support you with our hands rather than the walker. That way one of us will be on either side of you so you won't fall."

Again, they moved into position and turned to Susan. "Ready?" She nodded. "Yes."

They turned behind them to the nurse who was positioned on

the other side of the bed. "Okay, slowly raise the bed."

They told Susan to lean forward onto her legs. They grasped both of her arms and told her to stand.

"On both legs?" she asked.

"On both legs," they replied. "And if you feel like you can't do it, just sit right back down on the bed."

Susan steeled herself, and again the nurse started to raise the bed.

"Okay, lean forward and stand."

Susan breathed, then let her weight press against the floor. And with both therapists lifting her from the side, she pushed herself off the bed...

And she stood!

Yes, she was clutching for dear life to the therapists and looked about as straight and steady as a ninety-five-year-old *bubbe*, but she was standing! And it was remarkable, considering that her shattered pelvis, broken femur, and broken knee were only six weeks into healing.

She held it there for about ten seconds before the team lowered her back to the bed. She sat, rested for a few minutes, and then she did it again, and again...a total of four times, and it wasn't even the therapists who had suggested she try it a fourth time. It was Susan.

It's that determination that tells me that she will win this fight, that she will eventually get her wish and desire...

To return to her children, to her husband, to her home.

day 47

We really need to get into the Cedars rehab program.

This is an in-hospital program that is really fantastic, but with the extent of Susan's injuries, they're not sure she's ready for it yet. The problem is, she no longer needs the medical care and attention that she's currently getting, so staying where she is is no longer warranted. She's in injury limbo: too well to stay in the hospital and not functional enough to go into rehab.

Everyone's pulling for her to stay in the hospital a little longer, but it's also an insurance issue. Insurance won't cover the additional stay if it's not medically necessary, but if the hospital doesn't approve her for rehab, we have to find a sort of rehab halfway house where she can continue to recover until she's ready for the Cedars program.

In anticipation of her not getting approved, I met with a counselor who gave me a few options to check out. The best facility for her, though, is about forty miles away, which is not very attractive for me or anyone else. However, the counselor did say that this facility deals specifically with spinal injuries and has semiprivate rooms. The other options were closer, but she didn't think I'd find them as "attractive." She said that I should look at them, though, to be prepared, because once this goes down, it's going to go down quickly. Reviewing the list of possible facilities, I chose one that was close to Cedars, located in Beverly Hills. Supposedly, this was the nicest of the geographically desirable possibilities, so I made an appointment for Susan's mother and me to visit it.

The lobby was nice enough, but once we began touring the facility, I could immediately tell that it was more of a "senior" home than a rehab facility. For most of these residents, there was not going to be any recovery and return home. This was a final destination.

I asked to see a sleeping area, having seen up to this point only common rooms. The patient rooms were long, military-style barracks, about eight cot-like beds to a room with flimsy curtains dividing them. TVs blaring from each individual space competed with the varied, loud moans and cries for help. That's just what it looked and sounded like; the smell was equally horrific. It was an absolute nightmare. *This* is what the Cedars staff thought would be appropriate for Susan's next step of recovery? The truth is, I think Cedars really did know how horrible it was, but there just weren't many options.

How could I possibly put Susan in a place like this? This is the woman who had to keep the door in our *private* hospital room closed because of the volume of the televisions from some of the adjacent rooms. This is the woman who would kick nurses out if they entered wearing any kind of perfume, or even if they were chewing gum. I'm not saying that she's particularly picky or sensitive...okay, yes, I am saying exactly that, and the reality is she wouldn't last a day here.

We left, and after checking out another facility, which was equally dreadful, I came to the conclusion that if she didn't get into the hospital's rehab program, I'd have to bring her home, set up a hospital bed in the living room, and take care of her there.

She really had to get into the hospital's rehab program.

I began coaching her like I had for her swallowing tests, telling her that when she was interviewed for the program, she needed to say that she was ready to do this and was going to work extremely hard at it. Every patient is required to reach certain milestones every week in order to stay on longer (again, driven by insurance), and if she doesn't reach that milestone, whether that means walking twenty feet or sitting up for a certain amount of time, she'll be kicked out.

"You do *not* want to go to one of these other facilities," I told her.

By now, the days of being furious at Dr. McSegal were behind us, and she nodded, understanding the severity of the situation. But when the rehab doctor came to evaluate her, the first thing I noticed was that she was wearing a strong scent. Naturally, Susan noticed it as well. "Are you wearing perfume?" Susan asked her.

Oh, shit, I thought. Susan's going to kick her out of the room for wearing an offensive scent and that's gonna be the end of our rehab chances.

"It's lavender," the doctor responded.

My heart raced, anticipating the complaint. Then..."It's nice," Susan said.

"Do you like it?" the therapist asked.

"A lot," Susan said.

"Here, let me give you some. It's good for healing." The therapist came over and put a little dab right below Susan's nose. Susan deeply inhaled and seemed to relax a bit.

Thank God.

From there, Susan pled her case the best she could, turning on the charm, but mostly displaying her unbelievably positive attitude toward getting better. This didn't go unnoticed by the therapist, who made a few notes and squeezed Susan's arm warmly before exiting.

The only question was...would this Oscar-worthy performance be enough? Lord, I hoped so.

Susan lay there, waiting until she was sure the therapist was long gone before she finally said, "Oy, with that lavender. Can you get me a wipe so I can get that stink off of me?"

That's my girl.

day 48

As we wait for the in-house rehab decision, she continues to get stronger, both mentally and physically. And though the physical injuries are more apparent than the mental, there are still lingering cognitive issues that make it clear her brain is still healing along with the rest of her body. What's interesting, though, is that no matter how absurd some of her delusions and hallucinations sound when she says them out loud, they still feel like such real memories to her that she doesn't question them. It's not like she's remembering them like we remember dreams we've had. She's remembering them as if they were actual, very real experiences. It's as if I asked you to recount what you did today and then afterward told you that none of that had actually happened; it was all a dream.

"We don't really have a hospital wing attached to our garage?"

"No, honey."

"What about the submarine boat trip? That happened, didn't it?"

"Well, did we take this boat trip before the car accident?"

"No," she'd answer.

"And you've been here for six weeks straight, so when would it have happened?"

"Wow, I guess it didn't."

Some of it she laughs about, like when I told her she cursed out the nurse for shoving a cat up her nose, or tried to flick me away like an annoying bug, but mostly she tries to sort it out in her mind and process it, amazed by how the brain copes.

Physically, she continues to work hard, though somewhat discouraged by her own limitations. Like her life outside the hospital, with her positive attitude, she has won many fans inside as well. That's despite her inability to retain any of her nurses' names, referring to them with whatever name pops into her head. One of her nurses is Lourdes, and she'll call out to her, "Luealla, can you get me a blanket?" "Lawenga, can I have an ice chip?" I'll say, "Sweetheart, her name is Lourdes." And she'll say, "Oh, yeah, I'm sorry," and then two minutes later, "Magdalena, can I get some Tylenol?"

None of them take offense; in fact, they often leave the room with tears in their eyes from laughing. "She's funny, your wife." They're right, she is.

The nurses have found and appreciate Susan's unflinching honesty. And some can handle it better than others. Take the completely green, newbie volunteer who ventured into her room the other day and said, "Hello, I'm a volunteer with the hospital, and I was wondering if I could ask you a few questions about your stay here?"

"Sure," Susan said.

He studied his clipboard questionnaire and began.

"Okay, first...when people come into your room, do you notice them applying hand sanitizer?"

Susan paused for a moment and then responded, "Um, you may have noticed that I have this thing screwed into my head, which kind of keeps me from moving my head at all, so I really don't notice too much of what anyone is doing."

Embarrassed, the volunteer stood there for a moment, his pencil poised over paper, then excused himself, and slunk out of the room. That concluded the survey.

During physical therapy today, she was lifted by a kind of harness device before being placed in a wheelchair. We then took a nice stroll around the entire floor. We rolled along, Susan and I on our little date, stopping occasionally to appreciate the impressive art collection that lines the hospital walls, as well as for nurses and hospital staff to admire her progress, which she humbly dismissed.

Toward the end of the hall, we reached a large window and I turned her toward the sun. She closed her eyes and enjoyed the warmth on her face. This was the real world, the one she hadn't experienced for the past six weeks.

We eventually returned to her room, and as we stopped, I didn't realize I had parked her in front of her large bathroom mirror, where she saw her reflection for the first time. Up until now, I hadn't wanted to show her a picture or reflection for fear she might get freaked out by the halo. But she didn't. She just studied her image and said, "Wow." She wasn't horrified, just a little surprised.

She then stayed in the chair for about an hour until her physical therapist returned and told us they're thinking of moving her to the rehab floor as early as tomorrow. And while we're thrilled that it looks like we are going to be placed there, Susan immediately became fearful, concerned she wasn't going to be able to do it, that it would be too painful, that she would fail.

The therapist assured her that she was going to be fine. She was making great progress, and yes, it was going to be difficult and painful, but she knew without a doubt that Susan was up for it. Susan remains less convinced but understands that it's the next, inevitable, step.

So as we reach the end of this chapter and move into the next, I just watched her in that chair, clearly scared, and thought back to all she's battled to get to this point, the miraculous progress she makes every single day. And seeing her there, parked in front of that mirror, the insecurity on her face, I couldn't help but think...

Isn't it remarkable how someone can look at her own reflection but not actually see the person she truly is?

THE THIRD PART: REHAB

days 49–51

I remember weeks ago, when it came time to leave the ICU. That morning, the doctors had mentioned that she'd probably be moving soon and then, bam, three hours later we were rolling down the hospital corridor to our new destination.

Such was the case this morning when the final word came that we'd be moving to the rehab wing and entering that program! We had been anticipating the change, knowing it had been approved by the hospital, but just needed insurance to sign off. That came late last night, and this morning we were packing up and once again rolling down the corridors.

It wasn't long before she was settled into her new room and the assessments began, and by my account, it was a day of immense progress, exhausting, emotionally draining, but so, so positive. For Susan, it just reinforced what I've had seven weeks to mentally prepare myself for, what she now has to come to terms with as well: this long, bumpy road we're on.

Earlier in the day, she was asked what her goals are.

"To go home, to be with my husband, my babies, my friends. I want to go to parties again. I want to walk on the beach. I want what my life was." By the time she had finished, she was crying.

No one in the program said her goals were unrealistic, but no one said she'd be doing all that and more. They simply said, "Good."

When they had all finished for the day and it was just us alone, she looked at me with tears in her eyes and said, "This is so not my thing. I don't know if I can do it."

"But I do," I told her. "Listen, it's great to have the goals that you have, and those are my goals, too. We're going to get there, but focusing on that right now can seem so far away and impossible to reach. Instead, focus on what you did. You stood up, right? That's great, and maybe tomorrow or the next day, you'll take a step. And that's what we're going to do, take it one step at a time."

Earlier in the day, when talking about her rehab now and for the future, Dr. Allison had told her that it was all going to take time, reminding her, "Susan, your injuries were very...severe."

It was said in that same tone I've heard from some of her other doctors, again making me wonder what conversations they might have had about Susan in private, and for that matter, what they might still be having, conversations I don't really want to know about. Even my dear friend, the anesthesiologist at the Hospital for Special Surgery in New York, was surprised by how long it took her to snap out of her delusions. At the time, he never told me that it was going on longer than he thought it would or should, or that he was getting concerned. But now that she was out of it, he felt like he could tell me—just one example of those conversations that others were having about the severity of her condition.

"Okay, one step at a time." Susan breathed deeply, went silent for a moment, and then asked, "Do you think there's some reason why I'm still here?"

Another one of those questions that I've considered.

"Yes," I said.

"What is it?"

Even though I've considered the question, I hardly knew the answer. "Maybe we don't know yet."

She then looked at herself, her floppy right wrist, her left leg that can barely move on its own, again giving in to the enormity of the work ahead of her. "So, is this what my life is going to be?"

"No. This is what your life is now. But it's not what it's going to be."

And that was the end of the first day of the next chapter of this story.

the unposted: part 10

During the course of these first two months, there were so many days when the kids missed their mom, but few as much as this one.

Alyce came home from school and seemed unusually quiet. When I asked her if she was okay, she broke down in tears, again uttering those now familiar words, "I miss Mommy." Unlike the early days when Susan was unconscious, hooked to machines and unable to communicate, today I was able to ask Alyce if she wanted to call her.

With tears preventing speech, she nodded her head.

I dialed Susan's cell, which she picked up.

"Hi. Al's upset and wants to talk to you."

"Is she okay?"

"Yeah, she's just missing you."

I handed the phone off, and Al managed to choke out the words "Hi, Mommy" before wandering away from me for privacy. She spoke quietly for a few minutes in the other room before returning and handing me the phone.

"Is she okay?" I asked Susan.

"Yeah..." and then the emotional bombshell, "but she just got her first period. You're going to need to help her."

My heart ached—for both of them, really. It was an event

they were meant to share, one of life's mother/daughter milestones. But the accident had broken that promise. They both had been robbed; and neither would get this one back.

I took Alyce upstairs to the bathroom, reassuring her that everything was okay and that she could have told me. She said that she didn't think I'd know what to do. We walked to the bathroom cabinet where she brought out a box of pads she and Susan had bought together on one of their girl outings. "Mommy never showed me how to put it on."

Susan had prepared Alyce for the big event, and though Alyce was pretty developed for her age, being just twelve, Susan thought she still had a little more time and hadn't gotten around to showing her how to actually use the things. Naturally it was a bit foreign to me, but I took out one of the pads, removed the backing, and showed her how to place it on her underwear.

Alyce looked at me, puzzled, and asked, "How do you know how to do that?"

"I don't. Just pretending."

We smiled and I hugged her, both of us holding on tightly, silently reminded of how close we had come to this "single dad" moment becoming the norm. I was sad for Susan missing out on this experience, yet I couldn't help but feel grateful for simply having both Alyce and Susan here, and for this special moment in time with my daughter, even if it differed wildly from what we all had expected it to be.

There wasn't much these days that was how we had envisioned it, but I know that not many of us are able to accurately see our own futures. We can imagine, and we can even prepare, but ultimately, only time will tell exactly how it will play out.

As the expression goes...man plans and God laughs.

days 52–56

While she still doesn't see it as she completes her first week of rehab, the distance Susan has traveled is momentous. She just doesn't have perspective. She only recently woke up, and in her mind she should just be able to get out of bed and walk or eat or go to the bathroom or any one of the myriad activities most of us take for granted. Her ongoing inability to do these everyday things, as well as the pain she's experiencing, has naturally caused her to feel demoralized, depressed, and helpless.

"I can't do it. I can't do it."

"Stop! Breathe!"

"Okay, okay, don't yell at me."

"I'm not yelling, but you need to stop talking. Just breathe."

"Okay. I'll breathe. I'm breathing."

"You're still talking."

My God, the stream of words and sounds that continuously comes out of her. The "ohs" and "ahs" and "oh, boys" and "oys" and "ah, ah ahs." It's a constant and pretty hilarious. She hasn't even been in the program a week and already has an endearing reputation with the therapists, who find it all very amusing.

"What? You're laughing at me?" she playfully accuses them.

"No, you're doing great," they say, smiling.

She *is* doing great, and part of her knows it, beaming to the doctors on their rounds like a bragging toddler. "I did five transfers today" (from the bed to the wheelchair). "I stood for five minutes." "I did some yoga and relaxation exercises." And then, on a turn, so emotional and vulnerable, quickly dissolving into tears and confessing, "I'm trying. I want to do a good job so you won't kick me out."

And then there's that affectionate smile from them again. "We're not going to kick you out."

So day after day, Susan continues to face her fears and push herself, now visualizing just the positive, repeating to herself like a mantra, "Okay, I can do this. I can do this." And she can, and she does.

This was our week of Hanukkah, and as it concluded its eight days of miracles, I know I've experienced my own—Susan and Alyce surviving the accident, Susan beating the odds and making it through the numerous complications that could have done her in, and seeing how far she's come in these few short days of rehab.

To celebrate, on Sunday I brought Michael and Alyce in for our own little holiday party. The kids and I walked through the hospital halls carrying several boxes of wrapped presents and brought them into Susan's room. There, amid the smell of sanitizer and stuffy hospital blankets, the three of us crowded onto her bed while she sat in her wheelchair, and we opened presents. The kids forgot where they were or just didn't care, and seeing Susan watching their excited, smiling faces, neither did we.

We were together, our little family, and that's all that mattered.

days 57-61

The other morning Alyce came down to the kitchen and said, "I had a really good dream last night."

"What was it?"

"Well, Mama came home from the hospital and she was walking and drove us to school and then we cuddled at night...and it felt good."

Besides being a beautiful dream, in truth, we are getting closer to that dream becoming a reality—ironically, in some ways alarmingly sooner than we thought...the coming home part anyway.

Not that any one of us, including Susan, doesn't want her to be back home. It's been her driving force since the day she was first brought into the ER, but the discharge date from the hospital, currently scheduled for eleven short days from now, feels frighteningly close.

The other day her physical therapist gave her a list of what she'll need at home—a wheelchair, walker, shower seat, and possibly hospital bed. It became devastatingly clear to her that the notion she held of just getting up and walking out of the hospital was just a fantasy. "I just didn't have those expectations that that would be my life at home."

Dr. Allison responded gently but soberly, "You'd have to be superhuman to expect that you'd just shake all this off and walk out of here."

I stayed silent, but I was thinking, *She has been superhuman. Why should that change now?* As one of her therapists pointed out while working with her, "In all my time here, I've never seen some-one with as many broken bones as you."

When I consider the imminent discharge date, I confess it feels extremely unnerving. Maybe I'll be surprised by how quickly some things start to click and come together, but right now I'm standing in a remodel that's been gutted to the studs with a move-in date less than two weeks away. Perhaps that date will change, but we have to be ready if it doesn't, and we'll have the equivalent of sleeping bags, space heaters, and flashlights if that's what we have to do.

As part of that planning, Susan's neurosurgeon, Dr. Baron, called for another CT scan of her neck. When he came with the re-sults, he took me out into the hall and was very excited to show me how the bone is growing in. The "pictures" looked like ancient hi-eroglyphics—he lined up the original scan of her injury to one post-surgery, and then to the one from this morning, pointing at light areas of bone, dark areas of fractures, and bright areas of metal plates. He kept looking at me and saying, "See this? And look at this! And now look at this!"

I nodded and smiled like I do when anyone is speaking a for-eign language, but I did understand the gist: He was very pleased, and that's all I really cared about. No paralysis and very promising for a complete recovery.

Though the progress was extremely positive, unfortunately the halo has to stay on for another four weeks, and that's a bummer. We had hoped that when Dr. Baron saw the scan, he'd feel com-fortable removing it, but he's being conservative. So the albatross known as the "crown of thorns," as Susan refers to the screwed-in headpiece, will still be in place when she comes home. She took the news of its additional four weeks much better than simply in stride, and I still am amazed at her inconceivable ability to tolerate the confinement of the halo as well as she does.

Other than that, the time we've spent together during this re-hab period has largely been quiet and very sweet, except for a cou-ple of times she's felt Dr. McSegal has raised his controlling and lecturing head. I can't help but feel the pressure of her looming dis-charge date, but I have to be careful to not let my intended support and encouragement turn into pedantic task mastering.

I've also taken the opportunity to finally read to her the many, many cards she's received, which I've been holding on to until she could fully absorb them. With the majority of them, I'm only able to read a few lines before I have to stop, collect myself, and continue. What comes through collectively is the profound influence Susan has had on so many, and how wonderfully inspirational she is while being so, so loved.

To each, she responds, "Wow" or "How sweet," somehow continually surprised by the absolute pure affection and admiration that is held for her. And as I pull out the next one from the stack, I think to myself that maybe one day she'll get it...or then again, perhaps not.

And maybe that's part of the reason why there's so much affection there in the first place.

the unposted:
part 11

L ike that wave I experienced early on, just when you least expect it, something comes up and knocks you on your ass.

The other day, I was visiting an Aussie friend who invited me for tea. As we were talking, my cell phone rang. It was Susan, just checking in, and I stepped outside to chat with her for a few minutes. Just the day before, after reading to her the many cards she had received, I put them all in a big box, which she named the "box of love." When I got home that day, a book had arrived for me, sent from her high school class, who had all been following the updates on the class's Facebook page.

At this point in her recovery, Susan knew I was sending out the updates, but she hadn't yet read any of them. While I was writing them, there were many times when I grappled with the fear that I might be disclosing information she wasn't comfortable sharing. But the support we both received from these missives was so immense that I continued. They were written out of pure love, so where could the harm be in that?

And then this book arrived from her former classmates. I told Susan that members of her high school class had been very kind and supportive in emails to me, and that they had also sent a book. The book was about a mother who was dealing with a brain injury her child suffered following a skateboard accident. When I told Susan this, she exploded. "You told everyone I have a brain injury?! Why would you do that?!"

"Because you did."

"But everyone didn't need to know that!"

My heart sank and my head spun. In that moment, my mind ran through all the other updates I had written. What else had I shared that could be perceived as a betrayal of confidence?

She was furious, but this was a different anger than the delusional anger I had experienced. This anger was rational. I tried to explain that I had simply written about it as one of her injuries, like one of her broken bones that was now healing. And that her brain injury was also healing.

She wasn't having any of it, and, in that backyard of my friend's house, I lost it, trying to explain to her through sobs that all I've been trying to do is help her, take care of her, take care of the children, take care of myself. I was doing the best I could. "The last thing I would ever do is something to hurt you," I added.

Hearing my pain and frustration softened her. "I just don't want anyone to look at me differently or treat me differently."

"I understand. I'm sorry. They won't."

I didn't think they would. I hoped to God they wouldn't. All I could think about was the irony in this. These updates, written out of pure love, were going to become our marriage breaker, the cause of our divorce.

Following that phone call, Susan began reaching out to friends and asking them if she should be embarrassed about what I had been writing about. Fortunately, the response was a resounding "No."

Hearing this made me feel much better and helped my cause with her tremendously, but I also knew that it wouldn't be until Susan read what I had written that she would know it for herself to be true.

At least, I desperately hoped so.

days 62–64

"I'm walking! Oh, my God, I'm walking!"

Christmas arrived a couple days early for me when Susan gave us the gift of taking her first few steps. Supported by parallel bars, she stood seemingly much taller than ever and was even able to let go of the bars for a few seconds, standing freely on her legs. Full of conflicted emotion, recognizing how comparatively minuscule the steps were relative to the distance yet to travel, she tearfully acknowledged the enormity of the accomplishment.

After her exhilarating therapy session, now in the wheelchair, we left the hospital floor and ventured outside, Susan feeling the cool air on her face for the first time in two months, breathing in the fresh air. We strolled around the plaza area, enjoying a little walk together and talking. After a few minutes, I asked her where she'd like to go next, and in perfect form, she answered, "I don't know. Is there a gift shop?"

Back in her room, my brother and his girlfriend came to visit and we just sat and talked. If I closed my eyes, the conversation could've been going on in our living room or at dinner. I haven't been too worried about Susan's cognitive functions for at least a week now, and my lack of concern was further solidified with my enjoyment of just listening to her. She talked about her birthday, which fell on Yom Kippur this past year, just a few weeks before the accident, and how she spent a good part of her birthday in services. She mused, ironically reflecting about the holiday prayers…"I keep thinking about Yom Kippur, 'Who shall live and who shall die,' and who shall get hit by a bus."

Just like the rest of us, she too is grappling with the randomness of life and the bigger questions of "Why?" and "What if?" "What if I had just left a few minutes later?" But she doesn't dwell on trying to make sense of it or going back in time; rather, she simply states, "I can't believe I'm here." And in that one statement, she covers two meanings, "I can't believe this happened to me and landed me here," and "I can't believe I survived."

It's hard for all of us to believe.

Michael and Alyce left on Saturday to spend the holidays in Vermont with my mother and sister, Susan's injuries forcing her to ponder her future participation in a sport of which she was never much a fan. "I guess I won't be skiing again," she tells my brother.

"I don't see why not," says his girlfriend, referring to Susan's miraculous recovery.

"Yeah, but I don't see *why*," Susan retorts.

And I smile. She asks me, "What?"

"Nothing. You're funny." And she is, having a field day with the hospital staff when they suggest she decorate her halo for the re-hab floor Christmas party. "Oh, sure, drape a little tinsel around it and maybe some Christmas lights...and then just shoot me."

In fact, this year the rehab gathering would be the one holiday party we wound end up attending together. Making the best of the situation, Susan asked some of the other patients the equivalent of "What brings you here?" One patient, who was now up and walking, said that a horse sculpture had fallen on him and broken his back.

"Well, look at you. You're doing really well," Susan compli-mented.

"Thank you. I was actually having a hard time last week, but you really helped me," he said.

"Me? Really? How?"

"Well, I was thinking that I had it so bad...and then I saw you."

"Gee, thanks," Susan replied before taking a sip from her drink.... "What a great party."

He laughed and went on to explain that she had a great soul, and he thought that if she could have such a positive attitude with all she was going through, he should stop feeling so sorry for himself. So here was someone Susan had never even spoken to—maybe he saw her smile as she was wheeled to the gym or heard her laugh and joke from her room—and he was inspired by her en-ergy and love of life.

It made me think about this thing, a "positive attitude," and wonder if it's something you can choose to have or if it's hardwired. I do think you can choose to find and focus on "purpose," whether that's family, friends, goals, whatever will get you out of bed in the morning, and from that purpose a positive attitude is born. For Su-san, that purpose is her kids, her friends, her home, me, all the life she has ahead of her.

This is how we spent the day. Hardly the place we thought we'd be, but happy just the same. There was no Vermont snowfall out-side our window, but it absolutely was still very much Christmas.

days 65–67

She just keeps getting better and better every day.

Starting yesterday morning, I could immediately see that things were different. She had more energy, didn't "ooh" and "ahh" in pain when transferring from bed to wheelchair, and was just ready to go. When we got to the gym and she was wheeled onto the parallel-bar platform, she scooted herself forward in her chair, and with just the most minimal amount of guidance, lifted herself to a standing position, then gripped onto those metal bars and took step by little step until she had traveled the eight feet of the platform. She then sat herself back down into the wheelchair by herself, we wheeled back to the starting point, and she did it again.

It wasn't just the physical accomplishment that differentiated the day. It was the first day she really felt good about what she had done, really felt like she was making progress. She had been promised that the pain would diminish and that she'd get stronger, but it wasn't until she was able to experience the truth of that promise that she believed it. Now she has and sees that this journey back to her former self will one day come to an end.

She is so generous with her therapists, effusive with her appreciation and love for them, building bonds of friendship that are a mere two weeks young yet still indescribably deep. They get goose bumps watching her achievements, and while sometimes she poo-poos their praise, other times she tears up. "I did that, didn't I? I really did that!"

Yesterday marked the day her feeding tube, the G tube (or as Susan jokes, the U tube) was removed. At the bedside in her room, her doctor just pulled it out of her stomach with a pop. The hole will close by itself like the one in her throat did when they removed the trach, and since her catheter was also removed a couple of days ago, except for the halo, that's it; there's nothing left—no IV, no tubes, no stitches...just her.

Feeling elated from the day, I suggested we do some more exploring beyond the confines of the seventh floor. It was cold, but we bundled her up under a blanket in her wheelchair and ventured down in the elevators, first checking out the restaurant, then the gift shop, where she browsed some knickknacks, letting the feel of some clothing play against her fingers. We bought a few pieces of chocolate, which she ate with an ecstatic moan, and then continued on, finally sharing some French fries from the cafeteria.

It was our version of a foreign-holiday vacation, exploring this little town she hadn't yet seen. We strolled along the plaza, in no hurry to be somewhere or to get back, appreciating the simplicity of a French fry and a piece of chocolate like they were delicacies. We greeted passing strangers, stopped to take in some of the art, looked out onto the city lights. Just me and my girl, alone together, holding hands, on our oddly romantic date. And when she smiled at me, her eyes so full of love, and mine, too, we might as well have been on our honeymoon....

Albeit a destination to which we'd just as soon never return.

days 70-71

Neither Susan nor I have ever been New Year's Eve people. Growing up, I'd have skied during the day and been so exhausted that I'd barely make it to midnight. In the years with Susan BC (before children), there were no wild parties or elaborate send-offs of the previous year, no resolutions or particular "clean slate" feelings regarding the year ahead. Mostly, it was just another night, followed by just another day. Our perspective on the holiday continues to this day.

With the kids still away, Susan and I had our own little New Year's celebration in the hospital. I brought in some takeout, we wheeled ourselves into the seventh-floor dining/rec room, and as we satisfied Susan's Chinese-food craving, we looked back on the year. Over the past few days, we've both heard the same comment from different friends, "I bet you can't wait for this year to be over, huh?"

After opening our fortune cookies, Susan, locked in her halo, her broken body sitting in a wheelchair in the hospital where she's spent the past two months, said to me, "Well, you know, aside from this crazy accident, it's been a pretty good year, don't you think?"

If ever there was a statement that could sum up her optimism and view on life, this was it. She wasn't going to be defined by the accident, the pain, or the struggle. It didn't consume her, it didn't wipe away all that came before it or color all that is to come. As huge an event as it is, it was still kept in perspective to the rest of our lives, for which there is so much to look forward and be grateful.

After dinner, we went back to her room and watched a little television. At 9 p.m., we got texts from the kids celebrating the New Year. "Kiss Mom for us, tell her Happy New Year and that we love her." I did, we wished each other a Happy New Year, and at around 9:20, the nurse came in with Susan's nightly meds and we kissed goodnight.

Yesterday, her accomplishment was walking ten feet down the hall with a walker; today was twenty-five feet; tomorrow will be tomorrow. If time were measured simply as a whole, like the chunk of a year, how much would be missed in the steps we take each day and the countless moments that got us here, whether painful or joyous.

So we continue to move forward with hope, knowing that hope is tied to fear, just as strength is to weakness, relief to pain, healing to illness, joy to sorrow, and love to heartbreak and grief. All being perpetually linked, we choose to have both rather than neither.

For the past few years with the kids, we've gone to the same New Year's party, spending the night with dear friends. As part of the evening, we go around the table, together with all the children, and each come up with one word that encapsulates the year we're moving on from, and another word that projects the year ahead. It's a chance to stop and reflect and visualize, both backward and forward.

So after saying goodnight to Susan, I headed over to the party, where we continued the same ritual, albeit this year carrying more emotional weight than previous years. When it came time for me to share my word for this past year, I said, "appreciation." Appreciation for all the friends and family who have offered so much love and support, appreciation for all the good we have in our lives, and a deep, deep appreciation for the fact that it easily could have been so much worse.

My word for next year was "onward," for tomorrow, the beginning of another year, and more importantly and simply, for the beginning of just another day...a Happy New Day.

days 72-78

Her time in the hospital is rapidly coming to an end. Gulp.

A hospital bed is being delivered to our home, a friend built a little wheelchair ramp for our front step, the kids are excited, and we're definitely nearing the next chapter of this adventure—wonderful and scary...for all of us.

Susan is now able to walk for extended stretches with the walker and has even been able to ascend a stair or two. Whether she'll be able to make it up the stairs to the second floor of our house is a different story. That will remain to be seen once she gets home, but given her rate of improvement, even if she isn't able to ascend them now, it won't be long before she does.

In anticipation of her discharge, we even practiced getting into the car, which she was able to do without a problem. This alleviates the need for Medivans or other wheelchair transport, which comes as a nice relief and a reminder that that prophecy made months ago by one of our awfulizers would not be coming true.

When the departure day comes, in many ways Susan will walk out of the hospital as she imagined, baby step by baby step, favoring her right leg and a little hunched over, but remarkably, she will do it.

And then I will happily drive her...

Home.

the unposted:
part 12

How do you have the strength and stamina to keep going?

Around this time, this was one of the most common questions I was asked. The other was "What can we do to help?" The latter wasn't just empty politeness. Friends felt incredibly helpless; they couldn't visit Susan to keep her company; we had plenty of food; the kids were well cared for; another friend even sent her housekeeper over to clean the house for me. But they were anxious to do more.

In the grander scheme of things, in times of crisis, people show up for one another. We see it around the world when there's been a disaster—earthquake or fires or floods or devastating hurricanes. It's unfortunate that these things have to happen, but these horrible events do bring out the best in humanity, when we come to the aid of those in need. On a much smaller and personal scale, that is exactly how our community was showing up for us.

The funny thing is, when I would ask friends to just keep sending love and positive vibes, they felt that wasn't enough. "Of course we'll do that," they'd say, "but what can we *really* do?" Like the love and positive energy were just insignificant things.

What they didn't understand, especially for me, was how important they were, and, in fact, the answer to their first question. How did I keep my strength and stamina? When I sent out an update, and the next morning had a hundred emails in response telling me how moved they were by our circumstance, how it had made other husbands look at their own marriages, how others cherished and valued their families more, how people were forwarding my emails to friends of theirs who were also going through difficult times and found comfort through our situation, how others from all around the world, from every religion, were praying for us... that was exactly where I got my strength to continue.

This generous community let me know, every day, that I wasn't going through this alone, and I leaned on them for that. I tend to be a bit of a martyr and think, *Oh, I can handle this on my own. I don't need help.* But I did. I remember one day being at Alyce's school and running into the mom of one of Alyce's friends, who politely asked me how I was doing. Whatever was going on that day was particularly difficult, and even without knowing this woman very well, I found myself sobbing into her comforting shoulder. Though I think she got a bit more than she bargained for when she asked her simple question, we are now forever bonded by that moment.

The third question people often asked me was what drugs I was taking to keep me calm or let me sleep at night. I wasn't. I was soothed by the strength and love of others. I deeply appreciated how peopled showed up, in the very different but equally important ways they did. Sometimes in these times of crisis, the most important thing we can do is to remind one another that we are not alone. With or without a crisis or disaster, that's what we can do for one another. I for one know, there's nothing *little* about that at all.

It's everything.

day 84

About three weeks into all of this, while Susan was still in the ICU, a friend of mine wrote, "I so look forward to these updates...and to the day you no longer need to write them."

Now, eighty-four days after the first one, we have reached another milestone. Today was the day that Susan came home.

From the time she was first brought into the ER, through her battle, unconscious, in the ICU, the delusions that followed, and then all the days in rehab, her goal and desire has always been to get up and leave—to go home to be in her house, with her family, kissing her babies goodnight and lying beside me in our bed. And now, faster than so many believed possible, she has done that... well, except for the bed part. Currently she is set up downstairs in a hospital bed, but with her will, it won't be long before she ascends those twenty-two stairs and joins me upstairs.

When we first entered the rehab program, her doctors recommended that we tape pictures of the family up on the wall of her room, as motivation for what she was working for. When she was in the ICU and her post-surgery hospital rooms, I had done this for different reasons. In rehab, I never did. She didn't need it. That goal was so clear to her that it wasn't necessary to see it on the wall. In fact, perhaps having only that stark whiteboard with her daily schedule provided more motivation. I didn't bring in knickknacks or blankets and sheets to make it homier. It remained a hospital room, a place to want to leave. And leave, we have.

We know the journey is far from over. The road is long and there are huge challenges ahead. Hopefully, there will be no more uncertainty, no more setbacks, just steps forward. It's already quite clear from our first day back that it will require a tremendous amount of work and an equal amount of patience...from all of us. But that's the road we're on, and again, it's a thankful road we travel.

The halo will come off in a matter of weeks at most. When that happens, Susan will sit under the deliciousness of a hot shower and wash her hair probably several times over. Free of the halo's additional weight, she will become more and more mobile. The wheelchair will soon give way to just the walker, which will give way to crutches, then to a cane—this steady evolution, finally, will take us back to where she was before all this craziness.

It all still seems so surreal. The amount of time that's passed, nearly three months, simultaneously feels like years and like yesterday. Like life, full, and yet just a blip.

As I drove to the hospital this morning, knowing it was the last time I would be making the daily trip, all the excruciatingly painful details of where it began, the horrific images and events of that first day started to play in my memory. All in all, it was a terrible way to be reminded to be grateful—and an equally terrible way to be reminded how much you love someone.

Then my thoughts go to all of the incredible present and constant support, for which I am so, so appreciative. All the many prayers, here at home and as far reaching as around the world, always in spirit, the same, "Please, let her be well."

What continues to astonish me, and what Susan has still yet to realize, is how this has touched so many and in such a profound way. Part of it is because of who she is as a person, so full of life and spirit, but it goes beyond that. Perhaps it's also because of the randomness of the accident. She didn't do anything to cause it; she was just in the wrong place at the wrong time. Sometimes things just happen, and when they happen to someone we know, when they hit, both literally and figuratively, so close to home, it takes us out of ourselves and elicits pure selflessness. It can also cause us to plunge into ourselves, forcing us to look, to question, to savor, to appreciate, to value, to apologize, to forgive.

Our final day at the hospital and first day home wasn't marked by fanfare. I went to the hospital this morning like I have for the past so many weeks, but this time as I entered the parking lot, then the elevator, and then walking down the hall, I was truly relieved that it would be the last time. I found Susan in her room, in her wheelchair already dressed, ready to go. I packed up her clothes, our humidifier, creams, powders, and cleansers, placed them in plastic bags, filled out a little paperwork, and waited for her final discharge. A couple of her therapists, along with her lead rehab doctor, came in to say goodbye. There were smiles and hugs, but mostly just proud, proud eyes.

As a goodbye present, one of Susan's occupational therapists who had worked so hard to bring back the mobility in Susan's right hand, gave her a small steel mobile he'd made. It rests delicately on a fine point, precariously balanced, and so simply symbolizes a great deal: on a macro level, the delicate balance of that first day in the ER, the days following in the ICU, and then in the post-surgery ward. On another level, it represents the obvious delicate balance of our lives. The mobile will stay in our house always and serve as a constant visual reminder of that precariousness and fragility.

As we waited for our final escort down, Susan told me about the last therapy session she had, sort of a group exercise class with several other spinal injury patients. Each was supported by a walker and asked to sway back and forth, shifting weight from one leg to the other. Then suddenly in front of her, an older gentleman's pants gave way, dropping to the floor and giving Susan a frighteningly clear shot of it all. Some of the other participants noticed as well, but clinging to their walkers for support, none of them, including Susan, was in any position to do anything about it. So Susan, consistent with the other military references that have occurred during her recovery—from the army soup to the submarine rescue of the marines—took command for one last time and loudly called out, "Pants down. We've got pants down." Rescue came quickly and pants were restored, along with the gift of laughter that Susan brings wherever she goes.

When our nurse finally arrived, we happily left the room and the hospital floor behind. We wheeled ourselves to the parking lot and transferred easily into the car. We said goodbye to the nurse, put our parking ticket into the machine, the gate went up, and we were gone.

Driving away, she looked at me apprehensively and said, "Are we really going to be able to do this on our own?" With nothing but faith to go on, I told her we were going to be fine.

The rest of the ride home was fairly uneventful. Susan took in the sights like a tourist. I pulled into the garage and transferred her back into the wheelchair and then into our house.

She was very happy to be home.

An hour or so later, we had lunch and then spent the afternoon getting settled in. Our celebration that night was simply sitting around the kitchen table having dinner, all four of us, together again, the only difference being that Mom was in this weird contraption and pulled up to the table in a wheelchair.

Many have said to me that our lives have been forever changed by this event. But when I look at the fundamental aspects of our lives, they remain the same. We are all still here, still here for one another, and still gathered around the table for dinner and to share the events of our days. In that regard, our lives haven't been completely changed by this, but they have been shaped by it.

Toward the end of her hospital stay, Susan knew I was writing these updates, but she hasn't read any of them, nor has she seen any of the pictures of the accident or the news stories. Maybe in the future she will, reading about this character who isn't quite her but to whom she can uniquely relate. She's heard about the number of friends who have been traveling this journey with her, this tree of support that has branches we don't even know about. This one grand book club.

Susan has a real book club, which she adores. She loves surrounding herself with smart, funny, strong women and exchanging ideas. And she loves her friends, spending many hours a day nurturing those relationships. This new, other "club" that has existed for the past few months is a little bigger, but I hope Susan will come to appreciate that, through this accident, people from all over have come together day after day, sharing in this common experience, collectively moved and inspired by her story. It is the story, after all, of an extraordinary woman, who through her spirit and will, fought and triumphed against all odds and expectations. This woman who is loved, admired, and respected, however, remains blind to this and to the impact she has had on so many.

It's a miraculous story, one she probably would have loved reading. It just so happens that this one...is her story.

THE FOURTH PART: HOME AND BEYOND

the unposted:
part 13

I had actually intended for that to be the last update, feeling that it wrapped up things nicely, but friends emailed me asking to please not stop. In an odd way, it was like their favorite TV series had suddenly been canceled without warning and before it had a chance to reach its finale. And so I continued to write to keep us all connected.

Though Susan had spoken to a lot of friends by now, she actually had seen relatively few. For the first several weeks in the ICU, visitors weren't allowed at all. In recovery, she was still pretty out of it a good deal of the time, and so that period, too, wasn't conducive to visits. (Except when she was in her "angry" stage, I would purposefully have select people visit because she was always happy to see them, and it became a sort of deflective tactic on my part.) In rehab, she was either so busy or exhausted that she didn't really want to see anyone, and so now, arriving home, here was the chance for the visitor floodgates to open.

When people came to see her for the first time, they always entered the house a bit apprehensively, not knowing what to expect. The uneasiness of the "feeling out" period never lasted long, though, especially when Susan offered up her signature sense of humor. Comments like "I know...

you probably expected to find me drooling in the corner" were frequently met with a relieved burst of "Oh, thank God, you're still you!"

Because of the intensity of the event, I think a certain number of people did expect a change in her, not necessarily in personality but in her outlook on life. "How has this changed you?" they'd ask, like she now held the secret to the universe after being so close to death, or had been saved for some greater purpose. What she felt she was hearing from others was, "You've been given this great gift, this second chance. Now do something with it! Be better, be nicer, do more." It was never overtly stated this way, but kind of implied, and that's a tremendous amount of pressure to take on.

Yes, there are many out there who take out a new lease on life after having gone through a major ordeal, people who survive heart attacks or cancer or a plane crash, but I wonder if their new lease comes from confronting death with eyes wide open, staring it in the face. Susan thankfully doesn't remember the accident, doesn't remember the pain, doesn't remember much about being in the hospital at all—just kind of waking up and thinking, "What the hell happened?" Telling her that she almost died is processed with a fair amount of distance, like this whole thing happened to someone else. Of course, intellectually she understands and is grateful for how lucky she is, but she doesn't have the experiential memory to draw on, to give her that punch in the gut that oftentimes leads to these life epiphanies. It's a strange place to be.

In fact, that's one of the aspects of the accident that fascinates me. Susan lost about eight weeks of her life. She just doesn't remember them. The last thing she remembers is being on the phone in our kitchen and hanging up because it was time to take Alyce to school. That's it. None of the details about the accident at all. Alyce has little memory about it as well, though she does remember seeing the truck drift onto Hollywood Boulevard, the bus swerving as it approached it, and thinking, "This is not going to end well." She thinks she blacked out at the moment of impact and came to a few seconds later.

The brain is an amazing thing, shutting itself down as a protective device, instinctively knowing, "You don't have to experience this. I'm just gonna disconnect for a bit and I'll reboot when I think everything's clear again." It makes me wonder if that, ultimately, was the cause of Susan's delusions. When she was on pain meds, experiencing hallucinations made sense to me, but when she was off of them and was still having delusions, I wondered why. Could it be that in order to deal with all the pain and to focus entirely on her healing, her brain just disconnected? And was it that disconnect that led to the delusions? I don't have any real scientific proof for any of this, but if some expert told me, "Yes, that is exactly what happens," I wouldn't be surprised at all.

What a crazy thing to have to deal with. One minute you're sitting in your kitchen, and the next, you wake up in the hospital with so many broken bones and you have no idea what happened or how you got there. It began to make more sense when I think back to those early days in the ICU, when I would tell Susan what happened and her eyes would go wide. At the time, I interpreted her reaction as "Oh, my God, yes, I remember!" but really, I think it was "Holy shit, that's how I got here?!"

Yes, that's how she got here. And while she doesn't remember fighting for her life or begging for a drink or sitting up in bed or transferring to a wheelchair, she did all of those things. Now here at home, on the next leg of this journey, how fortunate to have made it this far and to have everything reconnected.

days 85–91:
week #1 at home

It's a girl!

Leaving the hospital with Susan, though larger in size and with greater communication skills, was eerily similar to when we left with our newborns: excited and anxious about what lay ahead.

Unable to get up the stairs, Susan's "bassinet" is a hospital bed set up in the living room, and even though she isn't in her own bed, she's happy—happy to be in the place she has been begging to return to for months.

And it's great to have her home. The kids love it, seeing her face when they leave for school in the morning and when they return in the afternoon. Our dinners together feel like they always have, Michael and Alyce excitedly talking about their days and Susan drinking in every moment. For the kids, the halo and wheelchair and scars are all invisible. All they see is their mom. And sitting there, the simplicity of having our family together again, picking up where we left off three months ago...well, I do stop and just smile. There is no turkey or stuffing, but every one of these nights feels like Thanksgiving.

At night, I go up to our bedroom, leaving Susan in hers. The baby monitor we had when the kids were infants has been updated to walkie-talkies. After a kiss goodnight, I place one on a table by her bed downstairs and the other by our bed upstairs. I turn my phone off, free from any more calls from the hospital, and turn the walkie-talkie on. Then, every night, whether midnight, one, or two and sometimes every couple of hours, the walkie comes to life and I hear a little voice on the other end, not inconsolably crying but rather uttering, "Gotta pee." Up I get, like I did with our babies, and go down to her.

In addition to bathroom needs, there are other middle-of-the-night calls. "Can you please get me some water?" "I can't find my glasses." "I dropped the remote." "I dropped it again. I'm so sorry," and so on. With each call, I can tell Susan doesn't want to bother me and feels bad for calling. For me, just like with a baby you love who is helpless, when they cry and need something, you do it.

Then there are naturally other times when the bathroom need

is more than just peeing. Between her broken arms, limited mobility and flexibility, she isn't able to reach around and wipe herself, so that has become my job, too. Humility and self-consciousness tend to fly out the window pretty quickly in times like this. Like many other women, when Susan and I first met, she wouldn't even fart in front of me, and now, twenty-five years later, here we are. Like the old Virginia Slims ads said, *We've come a long way, baby.* Again, we do what we need to do.

Before I'm nominated for any Mother Teresa award, you should know that I'm not a particularly happy nurse. I'll take care of the essentials, but when it comes to fetching and fluffing, I get impatient and intolerant. "Can you please get...I need some...Will you rub...Ow, my head is killing me." Each time I feel my patience wearing thin, I stop and look at her, screwed into that headpiece, scars running up and down every limb, and think about what she's endured. Even still, I find myself grumbling.

While we are beyond happy to be entering into the next phase of this adventure, it hasn't been without its own unexpected bumps in the adjustment road. For example: During the time Susan was in the hospital, the kids were forced to function more independently—bathing without being told to, cleaning their room, doing their homework without being prodded, all things that, previously, Susan primarily stayed on top of. In a lot of ways, their newfound self-reliance and independence was really healthy for them, even though it happened under the worst of circumstances. Now that Susan is back, she can't help falling into the same role she occupied just a few months earlier, that of "the enforcer." The kids not only don't need this, they resent it; they feel perfectly capable of doing what they need to do without being nagged about it. So in some ways, I think Susan is a little lost, trying to figure out what her role is now.

This huge developmental change with the kids occurred over a few months, but for her, there's been no gap in time. She expected to come home and simply pick up where she left off. But things have changed. The trouble is that rather than working to reestablish and redefine her role, Susan tends to try harder to force everyone and everything back into what they were before the accident, which causes the kids to push back, which causes her to push even harder. It's a vicious cycle that I finally had to talk to her about.

I told her how amazing the kids have been and that they didn't need the same things they did just a few months ago. "Because of all your lost time, I'm sure it feels like it was almost yesterday, but it's actually been a while and with a really steep learning curve. You have to give them some of the space they've become accustomed to having."

It's hard. In a little time, I'm sure we'll once again find our rhythm, but right now we're a little off.

Despite the daily appearance of new aches and pains, whether in her hip, her arm, or the splitting headaches she's been getting that originate at the pin sites, Susan, in terms of her rehab, continues to greatly improve. We take short walks around the neighborhood, venturing farther each day before she needs to take refuge in the wheelchair. The fresh air is so refreshing, but what she really remarks on are the colors, the green of the trees, the blue of the sky. Three months of institutional floors and walls have given her a huge appreciation of the beauty of nature, and she'll happily sit out front on the deck and call to neighbors as they walk by, each of them bounding over to greet her, tears in their eyes due not only to her survival but to her inviting smile and greeting.

As part of her home-nursing regime, she's been assigned a few different therapists to come by on a weekly basis. First is the cognitive therapist, who will help her get back to daily living, everything from going to the bathroom and washing herself to doing simple chores. Then there's a nurse, who will take her vitals and change any dressings. Lastly, a physical therapist will aid in getting her back on her feet. When the cognitive therapist arrived and Susan heard that she was there to help her relearn how to do things like the laundry and loading the dishwasher, Susan asked, "Oh, great. I bet my husband hired you to do this, didn't he? He's been complaining our entire marriage about how I load the dishwasher."

Despite our insurance covering these sessions, after only one visit from both the nurse and the cognitive therapist, we told them they didn't need to come back. Susan had already progressed past what they were there to help with. The physical therapist, though, was a different story.

While in the hospital's rehab, Susan found that using a tall pole was more effective than a cane for helping her get up stairs, so before she came home, I went to Home Depot and had a piece of PVC pipe cut into two six-foot lengths. I then put a rubber tip on both ends, creating a sort of large walking stick. Right now, she can manage only a few stairs at a time, but she's determined to build her stamina with the objective of eventually conquering them all. This ambition to make it to the second floor is driven by two desires: one, getting back into our bed; and, two, when her halo is eventually removed, finally reaching the nirvana of the oft-fantasized shower.

Dennis, her physical therapist, is helping her get there. Upon meeting her on the first day, like everyone who has reviewed Susan's medical records, he didn't know what to expect—perhaps someone writhing in pain, curled into a little ball unable and unwilling to move, possibly even unable to communicate at all from the brain injury. So when Dennis walked in, he nearly dropped in shock when he found Susan sitting up in her bed, greeting him with her trademark smile ready to go—in particular, wanting to head up the stairs toward the bedroom. He looked confused, like he had walked into the wrong home. He double-checked his clipboard, "Wait, you are the one who was hit by the bus, right?"

He told us that before arriving, his initial hope for her first day of therapy was to maybe, and that's maybe, get her to at least agree to try to do a transfer, perhaps take a couple of steps; but even then, based on her injuries, he wasn't going to insist. Instead, Susan was already on the move before he could even set his things down, trying to move her right leg off the side of the bed. As he moved to help her, Susan stopped and pointed out a stain on his shirt. "Dennis, um, what is that on your shirt?"

He confessed, a bit embarrassed, that before coming to us, he had stopped at the Rite Aid to get a chocolate ice cream cone and had a bit of an accident.

"Okay, well that's a little gross and you need to wipe it up."

She is anything but shy. Dennis, quickly realizing who was in charge here, dutifully complied. (It also gave Susan a much-needed parenting fix.)

In the couple of times we've now seen Dennis, his trademark phrase has become "You're doing very well." Susan hasn't reached the top of the stairs yet, but she is getting closer. If she pushed it, she could probably climb them all, but for now she's happy enough in her hospital bed in the living room, frightened that if she *were* able to get upstairs, she might not be able to get back down.

Friends often ask her how she is able to face the enormity of the recovery in front of her, adding comments like, "I really don't think I could deal." Her response, however, comes fairly easily. She tells them that as difficult as she knows her rehab will be, not trying was never an option. She also talks about when she was in the hospital how the doctors put the fear of God in her to get off pain meds as soon as possible. She can see what they meant, appreciating the danger of popping oxycodone and just lying in bed all day watching TV. "That's not what I want my life to be," she adds. "I want to have what I had."

If you ask her *what* got her through all of this, she'll say "love." If you ask others, they'll say "her attitude."

When I think about it, I wonder if the two work reciprocally— that the love she feels from others and for others is the source of her unflinchingly positive attitude, and that her bright, positive attitude is what makes others love her so much.

And despite all she's endured, Dennis is quite right...she really is doing very well.

days 92–98:
week #2 at home

My angel has lost her halo!

It was a day as hotly anticipated as Christmas, and there was only one gift on her list: remove this godforsaken contraption.

A couple of weeks ago when we made our follow-up appointment with our neurosurgeon, Dr. Baron, we had heard that he intended to remove the halo, but we weren't counting on it for fear of a huge disappointment if it didn't happen. Susan has been getting some very bad headaches that are now beginning to increase in frequency and pain. As I've noted, for the most part, she has tolerated the halo remarkably well, but even so, one can take only so much torture.

It isn't just being set free from the iron rods; she'll also be able to take her first shower in months. I think about how I feel if I haven't showered for just a few days, the itchy, greasy hair, the grime-covered skin. For Susan, this hasn't been going on for just a few days while on a camping trip or until the water comes back on; this has been months. Yes, she's had washcloth baths, for which I reach down the hard plastic of her body vest to wipe her down, feeling the knotted, now-stiff sheepskin fur or whatever that lining material is, but it's hardly satisfying. Keep in mind, this is the same woman who has been featured in hair product ads in beauty magazines for her long, curly hair, which has now turned into an oily dreadlock. I tried using dry shampoo on her, but that was about as effective as dry-cleaning a stray dog.

So I got her dressed and we headed to Dr. Baron's office with no idea what to expect. Do they put her under or sedate her to remove the halo? She hadn't been instructed not to eat or to prep in any manner, so that seemed doubtful. Either way, we didn't really care; we just wanted it done, however they do it.

When we arrived at the doctor's office, we were informed that the apparatus wouldn't be removed by our neurosurgeon but rather by "the appliance technician," a term that sounded frighteningly similar to a refrigerator repairman. Still, we wheeled Susan back into a small examination room and waited.

Finally, the door opened and the appliance technician entered. He was an older gentleman named Max, who was actually one of the inventors of the halo, and also the man who apparently had supervised the installation of Susan's. Upon entering, he informed us that his associate was supposed to have handled this appointment, and therefore Max didn't bring his tools. If we'd give him a minute, he was going to go back down to his car and see if he had a spare set. And then he was gone.

I began to joke, "A spare set in his car?! Is he going to get the tool kit the auto manufacturers include for incidental repairs?"

After a few minutes, he indeed returned carrying a little zip-up tool kit—exactly like you'd find packed with the car owner's manual and an emergency flare.

"Wait, you just do this yourself...with those?"

Without pausing, Max answered, "Yup," and took a little ratchet wrench out of the case and began unscrewing the bolts on the large plastic vest. Apparently my joke was no joke. Tackling the vest didn't seem too much of a problem. As far as the iron bars screwed into her head, I had no idea what he was going to do.

As he unscrewed the vest, and the looser it got, the more relief I could sense in Susan, until he finally pulled the pieces apart, freeing her from this primitive torture device. The first words out of Susan's mouth were those of pure relief. "Oh, my God..." quickly followed by..."I can't believe my own stink! Is that me?! Oh, my God, shoot me!"

Yeah, it was pretty bad. Despite the wipe-downs, we were only able to get her so clean, not to mention that the vest and its materials had taken on a life and smell of their own. We immediately wet some paper towels and performed a little sponge bath: back, underarms, gently on her neck. Her breasts are large, and she's well known for using them to function as a sort of secondary purse. Going out for the evening, she'll tuck lipstick down there, her phone—pretty much the entire contents of Mary Poppins's magic bag can be stored there. So here, as I lifted them to clean their underside, it was similar to turning over a large rock in the woods, unsure of what we might find. Fortunately, nothing living.

Free of the large plastic vest, Max then fitted her with a hard collar to stabilize her neck. The halo was still screwed into her head.

"What about this?" Susan asked, pointing to the metal bars.

"I'm going to do that next," Max replied.

"Right here?!"

Again, "Yup."

He reached back into his little tool kit, pulled out a torque screwdriver, and began attacking one of the screws, slowing twisting it counterclockwise, like her forehead was a piece of wood. Susan's eyes went wide, vocally accompanying each turn with an "Ahh."

I never knew how shallow or deep these screws were, but I imagined they'd be free with a couple of rotations, figuring they were superficial little stubby screws mainly there just to keep the halo in place. This was so not the case. As Max turned and turned and turned some more, it became unsettlingly apparent that these were major bolts roughly two inches long and screwed directly into her skull! They went on forever, and here he was, unscrewing them like Susan was a piece of IKEA furniture.

She said it didn't really hurt, but felt really, really strange. With our kids, she had had two C-sections, so she was familiar with doctors tugging on the insides of her body while she was numb, but this was a completely new level of bizarre. And, unlike with the birth of our children, I wasn't afforded the role of being just a horrified bystander. As Max removed the screws, I was tasked with holding the halo in place so that it wouldn't tip over, which, like a sconce in drywall, would have ripped the metal, threaded spikes right out of her head.

Finally, the first one came free, revealing at least an inch of depth into her skull. "Oh, my God!" Susan exclaimed.

Yeah, no shit, I thought. *There's a gigantic hole in her head!*

"They're easier to get out than to get in," Max casually offered.

Okay, interesting to know. "How *do* you get them in?" I asked. "Do you have to predrill?"

"No, I just use a torque screwdriver like this one. They go right into the bone."

Terrific.

I continued to hold the appliance in place, my arms tiring as Max removed the second, third, and finally fourth screw. He had trouble removing the back screws, as they were all knotted and stuck with matted hair, but eventually, accompanied by Susan's "Ows," "Ouches," and involuntary tears streaming down her cheeks, he finally succeeded in pulling those out, along with clumps of her greasy, bloody locks.

Then, with them all freed, he lifted the metal crown of thorns from her head. Blood slowly dripped down her forehead from the holes left behind, the imagery impossible to ignore.

"What happens now?" I asked. "Does she get stitched up?"

"No, the holes will close on their own."

I had seen how her trach hole had closed up like that, but I just couldn't imagine these closing in the same manner. After all, this wasn't just skin; it was bone, too.

"Just make sure to keep them clean," Max instructed.

"How do we do that?"

"A little hydrogen peroxide on a Q-tip and just clean around and in the hole."

"*In* the hole?" I confirmed.

These things disappeared like black vortexes into her skull, and I was supposed to stick a Q-tip in there and twirl it around? Max brought one out to demonstrate and then gave another to me to attack the next hole. Circling the opening and wiping away the blood was fine, but sticking it in there and twisting it around made my entire body cringe...just another one of many residual acts I never would have guessed in a million years I'd be performing.

For Susan, however, getting that thing off her head was a huge thrill. The next immediate task was to deal with her hair, which currently was a greasy, bloody, scabbed, and matted mess. We had brought a comb and brush with us, and at first I gently addressed the area, trying to coerce it into submission, but that quickly turned into an unrestrained assault. Making any progress on the snarled knots required pulling out large clumps of hair, which came out disturbingly easily...lots of it, handfuls that I discretely threw into the garbage to shield Susan from seeing how much she was losing. I was eventually able to get it somewhat under control and tie it into a small braid.

Meanwhile, Max had forgotten to bring the waterproof collar that would allow Susan to take a shower, so he headed back to his office to locate one. Once we were done here, we'd meet him there to pick it up, a stop we were definitely going to make before heading home.

A few minutes later, a nurse arrived to take Susan for some X-rays, and afterward we were required to fill out a questionnaire. Among other ridiculous questions, it included if Susan's back or neck pain prevented her from "exercising"? Yes... "driving"? Yes... "sleeping"? Yes... "sex"? Actually, it wasn't so much the back and neck pain that prevented the sex as much as the two broken arms, crushed hip, broken leg, not to mention the giant pot rack screwed into her head. Fortunately, Dr. Baron rescued us from our paperwork. He breezed in, asked us to follow him, and then just as quickly breezed out.

Before we were able to get up and maneuver ourselves out of the examination room, we had already lost him.

"Hello?" we called out into the maze of his office.

"Just follow my voice," he shouted back, but then went silent again.

"Okaaay...but you'll have to keep talking."

Like following an audible breadcrumb, we eventually found him in another exam room where he brought up Susan's X-rays to show us how she's been healing. After going through the X-ray-deciphering exercise once before, I was curious to see if they'd make any more sense to me now. They didn't. However, Susan, surprisingly, somehow seemed to be able to see exactly what he was talking about.

"Wow," she said as Dr. Baron showed her the initial X-ray of the break. He again pointed at these white spots, which he said were the detached bones from each side of the spinal cord. He then indicated how close each one came to severing the arteries that led to her brain, illustrating once again how very lucky she was not only to be alive but to not be paralyzed.

"Now I want to show you where we are today."

He pulled up another X-ray, which was dark and looked as foreign to me as the others. Again, Susan seemed to get it right away. "Wow! Look at that!" she exclaimed.

"Um...I haven't loaded in the X-ray yet," Dr. Baron flatly responded.

Okay, thank God it wasn't just me who had no idea what we were looking at.

He then made a couple of adjustments, and the picture came into focus. After his explanation, I could see that, yes, her spinal cord did look straighter and like bone was growing. This is what he was so excited about. Susan, however, was duly sobered by it all. "Geez, I was almost a goner, huh?"

Dr. Baron nodded, still fixated on the X-rays.

Then looking at the plate and screws in there, Susan tried to lighten the mood.

"They're gonna love me at airport security."

Dr. Baron didn't even crack a smile.

"You don't have much of a sense of humor, do you, Dr. Baron?"

"Trust me, you don't want a neurosurgeon who's not serious," he said.

Probably true. And if *good* meant we couldn't get *funny*, I think we all know which we'd prefer.

That was it, so we bid goodbye to another one of our miracle workers until our next follow-up appointment. I whisked Susan out of there, zipped over to Max's office to pick up the waterproof shower collar, and rushed home.

I wheeled her back up the ramp and into the house, where we grabbed her PVC walking sticks and began the journey upstairs, the huge incentive of a hot shower waiting for her at the top of the twenty-two steps. She managed the first three okay, then looked up at the next fourteen and deeply exhaled. I asked if she was okay and she nodded. As she stood there holding onto the handrail and the long stick, I quickly ran up and placed her shower chair on the next landing to create a makeshift resting station.

One by one, she began again, slow and steady, lifting her right leg and then bringing her left to meet it. I could tell she was getting tired, though. She'd never made it past the second landing before, but I knew that if we could get her up there, she could then get into our bed and wouldn't need to come back downstairs again until after she was able to rest and have a nap.

She finally reached the second landing, tired and breathless, and I carefully helped her into the waiting shower chair. She had only five remaining steps to get to the top, but these were like the final ascent to the peak of Everest. We've seen our share of mountain climbing documentaries in which hikers just couldn't take another step and lowered themselves onto the mountaintop only to perish in the cold. Here we were, on our own Everest, worried that if we waited much longer, she'd get too tired to stand back up, and then we'd really be screwed, stuck in that same kind of limbo.

While Susan was catching her breath, I returned downstairs, effortlessly sprinting down the entire flight of stairs without even thinking about it, in contrast to her struggle with each and every one of them. At the bottom, I grabbed her wheelchair and brought that up, placing it at the very top. If she could just make it there, I could wheel her into the bedroom and bathroom, where she'd only have to make the transfer from the wheelchair into the shower chair.

I returned to the second landing and asked if she was ready to continue. She nodded that she was. I helped her up, and we began the final five; I reminded her what awaited at the top. She didn't speak, just remained intensely focused on the first step, then the next and the next, until she finally summited and we placed her in the chair. There was no celebration, no flag-planting, just pure exhaustion.

I wheeled her into the bedroom, where she needed a few minutes to recover before even attempting the shower. In the meantime, I got her ready. I took off her shoes, her pants, and shirt and then carefully removed the hard collar, exposing her bare neck. While I attached the shower collar, I supported her head like an infant's, fearing its weight might just flop it over. I then ran the water until it flowed constant and hot, raining down in the empty stall.

Wet relief was just inches away. We got her to her feet, pulled off the rest of her clothes, and she carefully entered the shower. We have a stall with a separate bath, so fortunately she was able to walk right in. She stood for a moment, letting the hot water hit her back, bracing herself with her hands against the walls, an occasional moan or "Oh, my God" escaping her mouth. Then she lowered herself into the chair and asked for the shampoo. She lathered herself up, rinsed, and then immediately went at it again, working to rid herself of all that blood and dirt, washing off the event of three months ago.

After that second rinse, she was ready to come out. I wrapped her in a robe and got her seated again in front of the mirror. When I asked her how it felt, looking at her expectantly, she simply said, "Good."

Just good, I wondered? It wasn't the ecstatic response I was expecting. Maybe the climb to get here, the effort to do this simple act, was just physically and emotionally exhausting, even a little demoralizing, and that was the reason for the muted reaction. She explained that she was nervous and had a hard time really enjoying it. She was afraid of slipping and falling, and so, for both of us, I have to admit, it was a bit anticlimactic. (It would actually be the following day, her second shower, a little more settled down, that would be that "ahhhh" experience.)

As she sat there, I examined her head holes and could see that they were kind of oozing, so I took out the Q-tips and tried to coax out some of the goo. We had been warned that the holes in the back of her head were particularly prone to infection because the hair held more dirt, so I sifted through her hair to gain access to those.

Once those were cleaned, it was time to deal with her tangled hair. As I began trying to work my way through the knots and crud that even two washings couldn't remove, once again handfuls of her hair began coming out in my hands.

Susan's hair is one of her loveliest features, but now I could see patches of her scalp under what is normally such a thick mane. I don't know if this was because she had been laying on it for so long or because of the trauma of the accident or the amount of X-rays she's had to endure or a combination of all of the above, but stroke after stroke released more and more of it. There was no hiding it this time, and when we were finished, she had lost two softball-size clumps.

"My beautiful hair..." she said, weeping.

"I know... but it'll come back."

"Do you think?"

"Yes," I answered without hesitation, not based on any real knowledge, just hope.

I continued to work on her, but whereas in the past weeks I had run the comb through with complete disregard as to how much hair became a casualty of the tangles, I now found myself gingerly manipulating, trying to preserve as many of the precious locks as possible.

We replaced her waterproof collar with the hard one, and I again put her hair in a braid. Instead of her formerly thick, long cable, this one was thin and barely went over the top of her collar. The hair tie that previously was twisted and turned two or three times, now required four or five turns to hold the strands in place. Standing there, it occurred to me that her hair was symbolic of her recovery as a whole. She had lost so much of it, and it would take time to come back, millimeter by millimeter, mirroring the little steps she was physically taking until, who knows when, it would return to its thick, long luster.

After getting her dried off and lotioned up, I helped her into some pajamas and prepared to get her into our bed. She took the few steps to its side and lowered herself down. I lifted her legs up, she stretched out, and that's when I finally saw true satisfaction on her face. She lay back on the pillows with a blissful smile, and it wasn't long before she dropped off into a deep sleep.

It had been, when all was said and done, quite a day.

Generally, Susan's spirits remain extremely positive, she does have bouts when she still can't believe this happened to her and that this is her life right now. She knows it won't always be like this, but she wants it to be over already, the recovery part, that is. I have to agree.

We've been at this for close to one hundred days; it's a long time. She's also very conscious of her meds and wanting to wean off of them as soon as possible. Even though she's on such low doses, given the warnings she received while in the hospital, she is hyper-aware and slightly terrified of coming out of this whole thing with a drug dependency.

Meanwhile, just as Susan's energy hasn't waned, neither has that of our friends. The house remains full of flowers and other treats, and visitors remain a constant. Those who hadn't seen her in the hospital are amazed at how she looks and acts, and those who did visit her there are impressed by her progress. It's so incredible that just a few months ago, she was such a mess and that here she is now, still with no loss of any generosity of spirit. As one friend, who was going through some troubles of his own, was leaving from his visit, Susan said to him as only Susan can, "Let me know if you need anything!" The friend just shook his head and laughed at the irony.

One day, a friend came by bearing a hilarious gift—two six-packs of Diet Coke tied with a little bow. Susan still hasn't had a sip of this, the coveted drink (even though all her restrictions have been removed). To top off a really good week, I brought her a glass, a couple of ice cubes, and popped open the top to celebrate. She poured it into the glass where it foamed and fizzed, and then she took a long anticipated sip. I watched as she tasted, swallowed, and then uttered..."Ugh, this sucks."

"Really?" I asked, completely surprised by her reaction.

"Yes. I can't believe I wanted one of these so badly. It's terrible."

Sorry, Diet Coke. Guess you just lost your biggest endorser.

days 99–102

Life seems to be returning to normalcy...a little bit, anyway.

On Thursday, we had a follow-up appointment with our wonderful orthopedic surgeon, Dr. Allison. He, too, was extremely happy to see how well Susan was doing and told us that he had just been in a team meeting where Susan came up in conversation.

"Really, you all talk about me?" Susan asked.

He made an expression like, Are you kidding? "Of course we do. You're what we call a 'trauma victory,' " he said. "And we don't see many that reach the level you are, so yes, we talk about you often."

This made Susan smile—"trauma victory"—a little bit of notoriety, even if it comes from being hit by a bus.

For me, "trauma victory" is a title that inherently carries with it the flip side, the numerous and likely complications that could have easily turned victory into failure. Nevertheless, Susan's spirits were lifted hearing that she has been given this label. In the past, I've joked with her about some of the positive aspects about the accident. "You were on every major network; you were the talk of the town...and you lost a lot of weight! Your every dream come true!"

Now, coming from Dr. Allison, it was like he had just given her an award, one that we've known from the beginning she very much deserves and one she was also proud to receive. He confessed that at the time of the accident, he wasn't so sure she was going to make it; he added that many in her condition wouldn't have, crediting her strong survival instincts and positive attitude. I had heard that when trauma patients are initially admitted, they are given a mortality number by the hospital that indicates the likelihood of their survival. The higher the number, the lower the chance of living. I asked Dr. Allison if this was true, and he responded that it was. When I asked what Susan's number was, he paused and simply said, "It was high."

Susan then discussed some of the physical issues she's been experiencing. Despite working on trying to rotate her left arm, she still can't turn it past a vertical position. In addition, her hip feels locked in place, and she's been unable to straighten herself while standing. Then there's the swollen knee, swollen ankle, and ongoing numbness in her arm and leg, not to mention her Achilles heel and so on. Dr. Allison addressed all of the issues, half-speculating/half-hoping that the swelling would continue to reduce and that some of the nerve damage would heal, though he couldn't guarantee that the feeling in her leg and arm would return completely.

He did offer that her bones are "sticking" very well. He showed us the X-rays he had most recently taken, numerous plates, rods, and screws brightly lighting up the film in contrast to the dull white of bone. He then gave us the reason why Susan can't rotate her arm or stand up straight; both are due to heterotopic ossification, or HO. He explained that this is bone (or callous) growth that can develop around fractures. Strangely, for reasons doctors and scientists have yet to understand, HO, or this hyper-bone growth, is very common with people who have sustained a traumatic brain injury. They're trying to discover the reason for this so that they can artificially stimulate victims whose bones aren't healing as well and don't have the "benefit" of a brain injury for that extra boost. In Susan's case, she's sort of healed too well, creating excessive HO, which has caused her forearm bones to fuse, thus her inability to rotate her arm. The HO is also heavily surrounding her hip, which might be why she can't extend to a straight, upright position. However, he's hoping that with continued physical therapy, the mobility in both her arm and hip will get better. If it doesn't, especially in her hip, she'll need additional surgery. Great.

Armed with this latest information, we set a follow-up appointment for a month down the road and bid farewell for now. From the doctor's office, instead of heading directly home, we decided to make a stop at one of Susan's favorite places, Bloomingdale's! Even though she was confined to her wheelchair and didn't intend to try anything on, just being there, and the promise of returning in the future or visiting her many other favorite shopping haunts, put a smile on her face.

Life returning to normal.

For me, the return to normal has so much good to it, but as I settle back into the daily routine, ironically I'm experiencing a bit of loss as well. Like waking from a deep sleep and trying to hold on to a pleasant dream, I can feel any bit of spiritual epiphany I may have experienced slipping away. I've begun getting annoyed by traffic and lousy drivers again, frustrated by long lines, slow-moving people—all the small stuff I had learned to stop sweating. My state of "enlightenment" is quickly fading, like desperately trying to hold on to that relaxed feeling one has when returning from a wonderful vacation. I suppose it's unrealistic to never be bothered by life's little annoyances, and whenever my clarity seems to float just beyond memory's reach, the sight of a bus or the sound of a siren instantly reminds me of what could have been.

Throughout Susan's time in the hospital, we always pushed through, willing ourselves to get to the "light" on the other side. Yet it's so easy to bring myself to tears by allowing my mind to imagine the worst, for either Susan or Alyce, and wonder how one ever finds the light again after being plunged into that kind of dark loss.

I always marvel at the resilience of my grandmother, who in the course of her lifetime lost her parents, then her husband, then her son, and finally a grandson. She was still able to find joy in life. Susan continues to say that, even with feeling all the love, support, and prayers that surely guided her healing, if something had happened to Alyce, she doesn't know if she would have had the will to survive. I, too, wrestle with that one. My heart breaks for those who have experienced that kind of loss—who have to rely on hope and faith that that light will someday reappear, maybe never quite as brightly but enough to at least offer a glimmer in the otherwise tragic darkness.

And when I think about that, and what could have been, my normal is a pretty good place to be.

the unposted:
part 14

I finally took another job.

I was apprehensive about accepting it, but since Susan was doing pretty well and it had been about four months since my last paycheck, I needed to work, certainly more than I wanted to. The show itself wasn't that great, but given our financial situation, I wasn't in the position to be particular.

I said my goodbyes to Susan, leaving her as many instructions as when I left the sitter with our babies. It was probably unnecessary, as she had a stream of friends who were game to help in whatever way they could.

So off I went, very nervous. It felt completely strange that I was just going to pick up and return to work like the past months had never happened. Would I be able to stay focused? Would I be motivated enough? Even with shows I didn't particularly love, I always strived to make them the best I possibly could, putting my all into them.

When I arrived, I was faced with a different and completely unexpected situation. I hadn't worked for this production company before, and I quickly discovered that the guy I was working for was a complete jerk. When I interviewed for the job, I didn't have a great feeling about him, and within the first minutes of being there, I knew it was going to be a serious problem.

I struggled through the next few days, his attitude and personality not improving one iota. Every night I'd come home to what really mattered, and Susan could see the misery on my face. I'd had other tough jobs in the past, but in those cases, they were either physically demanding, or I was working extremely long hours because we were short-staffed, or I was dealing with constantly shifting creative. Nothing like what she was seeing now. I was demoralized, and it showed.

Over the weekend, I had lunch with a friend and confessed, "I'm not sure I can do it."

His response, knowing that I needed the work, "Tough it out."

It wasn't a matter *if* I could tough it out. Throughout my career I've worked for bosses who are considered some of the most challenging in the business. I respected them, however, and that made the difference. I've dealt with difficult writers, egotistical directors, and prima donna talent, so ultimately it wasn't a matter of *if* I could tough it out but *why* tough it out? What was I getting from this experience other than a much-needed paycheck, and while it might seem spoiled and entitled to even consider walking away from that, was it really worth trading in not just my happiness but also a bit of my soul? What I painfully learned firsthand from my father and brother and from the randomness of Susan's accident is that life is short—potentially, very easily and very suddenly, way too short. This was definitely falling into that category. If I hadn't just passed through this period of really examining what's important in life, maybe I would have had a different outlook. Maybe I wouldn't have reacted so strongly. I'm not sure that's better: getting stuck and numbed in a dissatisfying, crappy rut but not realizing you're even in one because you're never jolted out of it.

Meanwhile, by the end of the week I kissed the job good-bye and never looked back. Putting on my best Zen face, body, and spirit, I trusted that the universe would continue to take care of us.

At least I hoped to hell it would.

day 103

It was to be our first public outing, an event that had been on our calendar for weeks, another bat mitzvah.

Susan's excursions thus far generally have been limited to short walks and the doctor's office. Friends have been by the house for visits, but this would mark the official coming-out, and Susan wasn't sure she'd be up for it.

When she woke up this morning, however, I encouraged her to give it a go. I knew the friends who hadn't seen her (of which there were many) would be thrilled, and I also thought it would be good for her to take that step back into the social swing of things. Not that I had any concern that she might become agoraphobic or a hermit, but simply that it felt like a healthy next move. Still, she was nervous about people seeing her, especially her hair.

"Sweetheart, no one is going to care about your hair."

"But I care about my hair!"

I finally was able to convince her to go and proceeded to help her get ready, beginning with rebraiding her thin little tail of hair. We also made a deal that she could have only two clothing changes. Usually, for an event like this, by the time she was ready to leave, our closet floor would be ankle deep with the casualties of outfits she tried on and rejected, but since I was the one who had to dress her, I gave her just two attempts. We succeeded on the second one. She then did her own makeup sitting on the shower seat in front of the bathroom mirror, using both foundation and wisps of hair to cover up the still healing holes in her forehead, which for her were the most conspicuous and embarrassing of her scars.

We drove over to the temple, and I wheeled her inside to the entrance of the sanctuary. After parking the wheelchair, she used the walker to get to our seats. The service had already begun, so we tried to enter as unassumingly as possible. As you might imagine, that wasn't too successful. Almost immediately, friends who hadn't seen her yet lit up at the sight of her. They'd quietly rise from their seat and come over to give her a silent hug, tears flowing down their cheeks, the purest of love gleaming in their eyes. They'd squeeze her arm, partly out of support for what she's been through but also to touch the living example of this miracle, the action, in itself, somewhat holy.

Strangely, she is still surprised by the mass outpouring of warmth and emotion she constantly receives, whispering "Wow" to me after each visitor came by for a quick hello. As the service continued, the rabbi and I made eye contact, and he smiled and nodded hello to me from up on the bimah (stage). I smiled back and motioned with my head to the special guest sitting to my right. I could tell that he couldn't initially see Susan because the person in front of me was blocking his view, but as he maneuvered around them and saw her, he, too, lit up in delighted surprise.

During one of the songs, he took the opportunity to come down off the bimah into the congregation to Susan's seat. He knelt beside her, clasped her hand and whispered, "Is this the first time you've been back?"

"Yes," Susan responded.

"Can you come up for a special blessing later?"

"I suppose," she said.

"All right, I'll call you. So good to see you!"

As part of the service, the rabbi traditionally offers a prayer for the sick and healing. This prayer generally covers the congregation as a whole. However, if a member of the congregation has returned after suffering a particularly difficult trauma, they are invited up for a special blessing. In past services, we had witnessed others who have received this blessing and supported them from our seats. This time we found ourselves the receivers.

At the appropriate time, the rabbi called Susan's name, and as she rose from her seat and we slowly made our way toward the front of the sanctuary, he briefly described how she and Alyce had been involved in a terrible accident and that this was her first time back at temple since her miraculous recovery. As Susan made her way down the aisle, friends reached out their hands to touch her like they would the Torah when the bar mitzvah boy or girl parades it through the congregation during the service. Tears freely flowed, including my own, as she stood there and the rabbi blessed her, all of us collectively overcome by this sweet, powerful moment.

Following the service, we didn't stay long. Susan was tired and wanted to have enough energy for the party later that night. We went home, and she napped in the living room hospital bed for the afternoon. A few hours later, we once again rallied ourselves and made our way to the party. I wheeled her in and parked her at a table where she happily held court all night, once again laughing with friends, telling stories, getting filled in on all the gossip...her favorite place to be. She looked beautiful despite her thin little braid, which no one paid a stitch of attention to, or the little scabs on the front of her forehead, lightly covered by her blond wisps. All they saw was their Susan.

She was, without a doubt, the belle of this ball.

days 107–110

My baby's back in our bed again.

Up to this point, she's been sleeping downstairs in the hospital bed, because by the end of the day, it's too much for her to get up the stairs. But she's been getting stronger and stronger and was ready to make the transition. She got up the stairs (which every day she can handle better), changed into her nightshirt, and crawled into bed with an audible sigh of delight. I propped her up with pillows and she clicked on the TV, a smile beaming from her face. She's still on some sleep meds, and so after a few minutes she dropped off into sweet slumber. I didn't follow too far behind.

In the middle of the night, however, she had to pee, but unlike with the hospital bed, which she keeps tilted at an angle so that she can get in and out on her own, our bed is flat, so she couldn't lift herself out of it. I woke up, got out of bed, went around to her side, and pulled her up to a sitting position and off the bed. She used the walker to get to the bathroom, did her business, and came back to the bed, managing to sit and swing her legs back up on her own. Not bad at all.

Two hours later, however, when she had to pee again, I couldn't help thinking that, selfishly, maybe it would have been easier if she had just stayed downstairs. I'm sure this stage won't last long... hopefully anyway. Until then, I'll remain on the several-times-a-night-hoisting-her-out-of-bed peeing schedule.

Our social life has begun to return, and we had our first dinner out at a restaurant. We went with our friends Rob and Mimi, who coincidentally were the last people we had had dinner with before the accident. We arrived at the Chinese restaurant a few minutes before them and found the place packed. A few minutes later they arrived, but instead of wearing jeans or whatever for our casual little get-together, they were fully dressed in black-tie attire! Rob was wearing a tux; Mimi, a gown. And they had balloons for Susan and a present for me. It was a total red-carpet greeting.

I rifled through some tissue, opening their gift, and saw what I thought was a white apron. Mimi knew I liked to cook, so this wouldn't have been out of the question. When I fully pulled it out, I saw that it wasn't an apron at all, but rather a white doctor's coat... and there, embroidered on the lapel was the name "Dr. McSegal," and under it, a list of all my alter egos: "Lone Ranger," "Joe Shooter," "Turkey Joe," and "Captain Rogers." It was fantastic!

We spent the evening laughing, like no time had passed at all since our last gathering. At the same time, we recognized that even though little time had passed, much life had. On our previous date with Rob and Mimi, before the accident, we had talked about spending New Year's together. Those plans, of course, didn't materialize. When our waiter brought us our fortune cookies at the end of the meal, we thanked him and asked him why the restaurant seemed so unusually busy. He was surprised that we didn't know... it was Chinese New Year! So, as fortune would have it, we did get to celebrate New Year's together after all.

And now, as I write this, Susan sleeps peacefully beside me, her hand resting on my arm as she usually does, her little assurance that I'm still here.

And me feeling the comfort that she is, too.

day 115

Valentine's Day.

What could be better than having dinner with three of the people I love more than any other—my wife and two children—all of us laughing and recounting various memories from the past four months. The anecdotes are becoming just that, stories about a time that is thankfully beginning to feel like a distant memory.

Alyce reminded me of one that I had forgotten. She said, "Mom, do you remember Lipton?"

Susan laughed and said, "No, who's Lipton?"

There actually never was a Lipton, but when Susan needed to be shifted in her bed, they called in the "lift team" to assist the nurses. Susan misheard it, so whenever she wanted to be moved, she'd say, "I need to move. Can you please call Lipton?" And when the lift team arrived, she'd turn to one of them and say, "Thank God you're here, Lipton, I need to move." They never bothered to correct her.

Michael shared his recollection of first visiting Susan in the hospital. "You were really mean to Dad, Mom." I hadn't remembered that from his visit but was reminded that when I wouldn't give Susan an ice chip, I was angrily relegated to the other side of the room while she happily talked to her boy, asking *him* for an ice chip before then asking him to help her "get the carousel out of her bedside table," whatever that meant. Michael hadn't appeared too bothered by her anger at the time, but it's clearly something that stuck with him. He also remembered, "Dad was doing everything, Mom, and you were so mad at him."

Susan apologized, admitting that she didn't realize what she was doing or saying, and even when I reiterated that as being true, I could tell that Michael was still upset by it. It clearly affected him. He knew it wasn't fair treatment, and despite the excuse that her brain just wasn't working right, it wasn't enough to remove the abusive sting. He was defending his dad, and as much as I would have preferred that he had never seen the behavior in the first place, I was touched by his concern for me. It also made me appreciate how lucky we are that this was not something they had to experience under normal circumstances. I can't imagine the long-standing negative impact on kids who have to live in an abusive environment every day.

In any case, there undoubtedly was some residual injury that both Michael and Alyce had experienced. I remember a few weeks into the accident and having a sit-down with them to make sure they were doing okay. They told me they were, but they did have some complaints:

#1. "You're always on your phone."

#2. "You're always in the same mood." When I asked them what mood that was, they told me that it was the same mood I have when I need to get a lot of work done—super serious and not really paying attention to anything else.

#3. "You don't laugh and play with us like you used to. *You're just not as much fun as you used to be.*"

My initial impulse was to respond with, "Of course I'm not as much fun! Do you realize what I'm going through?!" But from the get-go, it had also been my desire to maintain as much of a sense of normalcy as possible when I was with them at home. To a large degree I had succeeded, and their willingness to unabashedly share their complaints with me was kind of a twisted example of that success; they had been somewhat shielded by the ongoing seriousness, complications, life and death, back and forth that kept the rest of us on the edge of our seats with a nervous pit in our stomachs.

Rather than become defensive, I copped to it all. I told them that I would put my phone away when I was with them unless it was the hospital calling. Deal. I told them that I *have* been distracted by everything that's been going on and will try to be more present. And lastly, I told them that I'd try to have more fun. Ultimately, that was the most heartbreaking to hear; as simple and obvious as it was, I had lost a lightness of spirit.

To prove that I could regain it, that night we played a rousing game of WrestleMania, the goal of the competition being to pin me down, sit on my head, and then fart. They succeeded in their mission, winning the contest, but for all of us, the laughter it generated was the real prize.

For me, the lesson was clearly learned. They knew that a huge priority for me was Susan and her health...but when I was with them, they wanted their dad. Thankfully, now, sitting around our Valentine's Day dinner table, they have both of us. Before dinner was over, they did ask for one more thing...

"Mom, remember those puppies you thought you got us? Do you think we can get one for real?"

day 128

We're taking yet another step forward.

Mile after mile on our journey, this new territory we're about to enter is outpatient care, having exhausted our insurance allowance of home health care. We're both sorry to see Dennis go, having grown quite fond of his commitment to Susan's recovery. Like a teacher gravitates to a passionate student, I think health care professionals must be similar, or at least Dennis was with Susan. Instead of our allotted forty-five minutes, he'd end up spending upward of two hours with her, encouraged and personally rewarded by her progress.

That has come to an end, and now she'll need to continue with an outside facility. From several friends we've gotten recommendations for other therapists who fall into what I'll call the "brisket principle"—everybody loves theirs the best, and we absolutely *must* try it. We'll probably end up checking out a few different ones to see who Susan responds to and who seems to be getting positive results. Though Susan is getting stronger and working hard, she still can't fully straighten, as her hip has her locked into a slightly bent position.

All the movement is in a positive direction, but it would be a lie to say that the voyage isn't becoming tiresome. I'm tired—tired of all the schlepping around and caregiving. Just as Susan wonders if this is what her life is going to be now, an ongoing regime of recovery and therapy, I wonder the same thing. Will we ever get back to where we were, and will it, or she, ever be the same?

Just after Susan's accident, a friend of a friend and her husband reached out to me. We had never met, but like many in the community, they had been dramatically moved by the event. This was especially true for them because they had been involved in a car accident of their own in which the wife also suffered a broken neck. After her accident, she, too, was confined to a halo, but in her case had a miserable experience in it. She became extremely claustrophobic, so much so that she needed to be medicated. (Hearing her story is what prepared me for Susan to have that trouble as well.) Initially paralyzed from the neck down, she put in a great deal of hard work and, miraculously, is walking again.

What was interesting, now that they were finally meeting, other than sharing various stories and commonalities, was seeing how inspired Susan was by this woman and, conversely, how inspired this woman was by Susan. Each saw such enviable gifts of strength in the other, minimizing their own situation compared to what the other went through. The friend commented, "I only broke my wrist in addition to my neck, and I know how difficult it was for me to rehab just that. You broke everything!"

Susan replied, "But you were paralyzed from the neck down and are now walking again! How amazing is that?!"

Both have experienced pain and hardship that no one deserves, and each was still taking steps toward recovery, steps that involve digging deep to find the required strength. Sometimes, as we experienced with this friend, it's hard for us to see just how far we've come or how strong or inspirational we are unless it's through the eyes of others.

That certainly has renewed my strength to keep up the fight and walk with faith that we're continuing to move in the right direction.

the unposted:
part 15

One step forward, two steps back.

Susan was taking it day by day but was growing tired of waking up without signs of marked improvement in either her hip or with her various aches and pains. If she knew for sure that there was a pot at the end of this murky rainbow, then that would be one thing, but she didn't. The pain could follow her for the rest of her life, and the thing I worried most about was that it would eventually chip away at her spirit.

She continued her physical therapy, but even though she was working hard and they were working hard on her, she still couldn't stand up straight, and that was discouraging. Some of her PT was particularly aggressive, and though she could always handle a strong massage, there were times I was really worried that the therapist was going to break her hip in an effort to free it up.

Another visit to Dr. Allison and another set of X-rays confirmed the continued existence of the heterotopic ossification. He was now expressing concern that the HO was indeed what was restricting her movement. He had previously hoped that it was only tight muscles, tendons, and ligaments, and that she might be able to work through those issues, but that doesn't seem to be the case. The solution would be to surgically go in and cut away the excess bone to free up movement, but he wanted to monitor it for another month or so more before we made the decision to go back in. If she could avoid more surgery, he (and we) would prefer it.

Susan expressed her frustration about her pain and lack of progress, and Dr. Allison reminded her that it's been less than six months and that people with these kinds of injuries typically take at least a year to heal. While that was reinforcing to hear, it wasn't completely encouraging in terms of the long period of recovery time still ahead of her. She wanted it to go faster.

On a more positive note, the visit to Dr. Baron, our neurosurgeon, went much better. Susan was sick of the hard collar she was still required to wear and was hoping he would liberate her from it. She felt that her neck was strong, and her own self-diagnosis was that she could do without it. It was my opportunity to now say to her, "Yes, Dr. McSegal, but let's see what Dr. Baron has to say about it."

Dr. Baron did another CT scan and returned with the news that she had fusion, but he would still like her to wear the collar for another month. Of course Susan was happy to hear that the break had healed so well, but she was disappointed in the additional month's prescription of the uncomfortable neck brace. So, what did she do? Well, when Dr. Baron said, "One more month," Susan did what she does best...negotiate, and responded with, "No, I think it can come off today. My neck feels strong." Dr. Baron looked at the X-rays again, and while I expected him at best to maybe cut the time down to say two weeks, he turned to her and said, "Okay. You can go naked...around your neck, that is."

Wait...aside from the masterful negotiating, was this a joke from our typically stone-faced neurosurgeon? Even the nurse seemed a little surprised by the out-of-character remark.

Susan laughed and of course said what we were all thinking, "Oh, my God, Dr. Baron, did you just make a joke?" He seemed a little embarrassed, but smiled. "I'm proud of you," she continued. "See, you can be serious and still have a sense of humor."

Which is exactly the attitude I hope she'll be able to hold on to herself, and losing the neck brace was a much-needed morale boost. From Susan's perspective, the rest of her physical progress might seem either halted or even reduced a bit, but by stripping away the collar, one more piece of the ordeal has been left behind, and that comes with tremendous satisfaction.

And that, I guess, is what a simple step forward looks like.

day 166

Well, we finally had sex again...if that's what you can call it.

Imagine combining the awkwardness of virginal teenagers with aliens who suddenly find themselves inhabiting human bodies with absolutely no idea about what sex is or how to do it. That about sums up the experience. The desire was there, but it was like a geometry problem figuring, out how to execute it. I couldn't really put any pressure on Susan's body because of her aches and pains. She couldn't get on her knees because they were broken, or lie on her stomach, or even spread her legs very far due to the restrictions in her hip. But it was the night before our wedding anniversary, and we were determined and finally found a position that worked...sort of.

The next question, while engaged in this unwieldy position, was whether the pain from the intense cramping in my calf was going to become too much to bear before I finished? Though it was nice to share that intimacy again, physically it was more uncomfortable than pleasurable and frankly a bit depressing.

Like all the other ways we were looking at Susan's future physical limitations, we were forced to examine this one as well. I had taken home a pamphlet from the hospital that suggested sexual positions for patients with back injuries. After reviewing it, it didn't come close to being applicable given the unique nature and scope of Susan's injuries, and I have a feeling I'll have trouble finding the pamphlet that pertains to our situation, the one titled "The simple guide to sex after you've been hit by a bus." Page 1: Don't bother trying. Hopefully, as she continues to get better, this, too, will follow.

Until then, that leaves us on our own, two aliens in these strange bodies, trying our best to figure out how they fit together.

day 215

On the road again...she just couldn't wait to get back on the road again.

Remarkable as it may seem, Susan got the sign-off from her doctors to begin driving again, just seven months after the accident.

I was concerned that she'd have the physical and mental ability to do so, but in terms of the physical, she passed her eye exam, and both her rehab doctor and Dr. Allison agreed that, even with her mobility limitations, she could drive if she wanted to. She does, and doesn't feel nervous about it at all. Fortunately, because she doesn't remember anything from the accident, she doesn't have any real PTSD to deal with...at least that we know of. I do worry, however, that perhaps some of that darkness lives inside her, deeply recessed in her brain and waiting to rear its ugly head as soon as she gets behind the wheel.

A month or so ago, we went to the movies, and there was a scene with a car chase that ended in a head-on collision. It was pretty disturbing, and when I glanced over to see how she was handling it, she seemed to be okay. Afterward, I asked her how she felt, and she said that the scene definitely gave her a pit in her stomach and was difficult to watch, but there were no residual images that flashed through her mind. In all this time, she's never had a single nightmare in which she relives the accident.

Given her clean bill of health, later that afternoon, she surprised Alyce by picking her up from school. As soon as Alyce got into the car, Susan burst into tears, grateful to be able to participate in this daily activity again, one that many perceive to be a nuisance or a mindless chore at best. For Susan, to be able to be with her girl again and hear about her day as they drove home together was now one of life's great gifts.

However, though Susan wasn't nervous about driving, I can't say the same for Alyce. At the time of the accident, Alyce was seated in the front seat of the car, and so for a couple of weeks after when anyone drove her, she opted to ride in the back seat. For a period of time, she also wanted to take a different route to school than she had taken that fateful morning. All understandable requests. Over time, she returned to riding in the front and was even fine with the old route, though she continues to clench at the sight of a truck or a bus. Hell, I do as well. Now with Susan driving again, Alyce has reverted to the back seat, just for that added measure of comfort and safety. But this first drive went smoothly, and I feel confident that her nerves will calm in time.

For Susan, having the independence that driving brings is huge. She's felt like such a burden all these months, having to be lifted and pushed and transported, unable to do really anything on her own. One of her concerns is that it will all become too much for me and the weight of that load will cause me to bail. As often as I reassure her that that will never happen, it hasn't lifted that heaviness.

Now, perhaps, as she returns to the road, in addition to the freedom that being able to drive brings, those fears will be set free as well.

day 282

I brought Susan to see the car today, or I should say, what remains of it.

Due to the ongoing investigation into the accident, it's been kept in storage for all this time. However, we were now told it could be released, and so I wanted to retrieve any personal belongings before it was sent to the crusher. Initially, Susan wasn't sure whether she wanted to see it, yet part of her was intrigued. By now she had seen pictures of the accident, which were met with incredulous horror. I was apprehensive about the visit, namely because I

Driver's seat   Alyce's little pocket of safety —
                                 front passenger seat

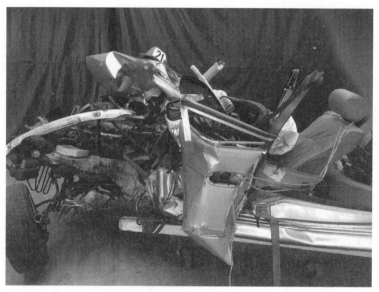

Driver's side profile

View from head-on — favoring the driver's side

Susan at the driver's side door

had already seen the car and knew that the pictures really didn't do the magnitude of the miracle justice.

We walked into the warehouse, and seeing the car in person, her mouth dropped and she began to cry. "Wow," was all she could utter.

She walked around it, amazed at the extent of the damage. Reaching the right side, she looked at the tiny pocket of space that used to be the front passenger seat and shook her head in disbelief. "How did Alyce ever survive that? And without even a single broken bone?!"

"I don't know," I answered, equally mystified.

We sifted around the remains for her favorite hat, the one so famously visible from the accident helicopter shot, but it wasn't there. We also checked the trunk for anything of value, sentimental or monetary, but there really wasn't much.

Susan then posed for a few pictures before we told the investigator who let us in that we were ready to go. She turned to him and said, "I was hit by a bus."

"I know," he said. "But finish the sentence."

"What do you mean?" Susan asked.

"Finish the sentence. You were hit by a bus..."

Susan remained quiet, still puzzled.

..."And lived to tell about it," he finished it for her.

Susan nodded her head, thoughtfully. "You're right," she responded.

He then told us that in the thirty-one years that he's been an investigator, and the decades he was in law enforcement before that, he's seen a lot of wrecks, but none that were this bad. "And to be sitting here, talking to you, after you were in there..." he trailed off, now barely able to finish *his* sentence. "That doesn't happen. Someone was surely looking after you."

I took in his words, which I had heard from so many others before him, and taking one last look at the car, how absolutely decimated it was, I found it difficult to not come to the same conclusion.

day 365:
an anniversary of sorts

One year ago tonight I went to bed and, like the rest of us, didn't know what tomorrow would bring.

It ended up bringing the horrible beauty of life, unpredictable, flawed and fragile, ugly and painful...and, at the same time, full of love, compassion, tears, and smiles. It tested strength and reinforced relationships, united friends and family, and reminded so many to be grateful for so many different things.

Here we are one year later, a very long year later, and I'm faced with simultaneously wanting to remember and wanting to forget. I want to remember to care where I should, and to not where it's trivial. I want to remember to appreciate, be thankful, and not take days for granted, even as challenging as those days may be. I want to remember to remember.

But I also want to forget—forget the pain, the fear, the anxiety, the smell of antiseptic gel.

So on this anniversary of sorts, this commemoration, that's the balance I live in, this dance of trying to remember and forget. Still, as hard as one can try to forget, the scars are constant reminders, some more visible than others.

Susan is spared the scar of the memory of the accident, but her body wears the scars of the trauma. I hope that someday, if not now, she'll be able to look at those scars with a sense of pride that she had the strength and resilience to survive against all odds. Alyce's and Michael's scars are less obvious, which can be more concerning because it's difficult to know how deep they go.

Thinking about the anniversary, yesterday Alyce said to me, "Do I have to go to school tomorrow?"

"Yes, baby, you do," I replied.

"Well, can you drive me instead of Mom?"

"Sure."

"And can we go a different way?"

So we took a different route, even though I knew that was just a temporary cure and wouldn't remove the lingering fear. We are all condemned to live with each of our scars, but we hope they'll continue to fade or that, in time, we won't look at them as flaws.

Recently, I attended the funeral of a friend, someone who had reached out to Susan at the time of the accident, who had been so very supportive and sweet...and was now gone. It wasn't lost on me how easily I could have been the husband in the front row of the chapel, saying goodbye to his love and the mother of their children.

The service was understandably tragically sad, but right afterward something happened that brought a little light to the day. A friend I hadn't seen in many years approached me and told me how she has been riveted by Susan's story, and that she isn't the only one in her family following it; her teenage daughter has read every update. The mom reminded me that her daughter is on the autism spectrum and that, throughout her life, her daughter has faced certain fears and anxieties. And then she told me, with tears in her eyes, "You have to know how Susan's story has affected her." She told me that her daughter, when faced with something particularly daunting in her own life will now say, "If Susan Segal can do it, so can I." This has become her mantra of sorts, to look at someone else's unimaginable challenge and use it to push through her own. It was deeply moving and inspiring for me to hear this, and it illustrated so clearly how something very good can come from something very bad.

Meanwhile, as we try to continue moving forward, yesterday we experienced another setback. Susan and I went to see Dr. Allison, who after reviewing her latest X-rays has sadly determined that she does indeed require more surgery. We had hoped her immobility would be worked out through rehab, but that's not going to be the case, and so she will be going back into the hospital in the next few weeks for what will hopefully be our last operation and our final stretch of recovery. Neither of us is particularly looking forward to it, but at the same time, if it's necessary, we want to get it over and done with.

In one sense, this surgery will be far less of an ordeal than what Susan went through before, but in other ways, it could be harder. This time, she will be forced to face it and the subsequent pain with a lucid mind versus her previous fantastical experience of submarines and sewing fish. Going into this, though, she is comforted by the thought, one you may have heard her say because she says it often (but also means it): *Love is the answer.* She's felt it all along from each and every one of you, this wonderfully large community, and she feels it still. For that, I remember to be truly grateful.

So as this year comes to a close, like always, we'll just have to see what tomorrow brings...

days 421–423: a familiar scene

Not exactly the place she thought she'd get recognized.

Here we were again on the eighth floor of Cedars, the same floor as Susan's rehab, but roughly one year later. It was eight in the morning, and Susan's surgery was scheduled for 9:30. While we were waiting to be brought into prep, it was like a bizarre reunion. As doctors, nurses, therapists, and staff passed by, when they saw Susan, they exclaimed, "Susan! Oh, my God! Look at you!"

She'd fill them in on her progress and explain why we were back, to which all of them were incredibly encouraging, echoing other previous comments we've heard. "I'm sure you'll be fine. If you could make it through all the other..."

Clearly she was a patient who had made a huge impression. Doctors and nurses who hadn't even dealt with Susan came by to say, "So you're the one. There's been a lot of conversation about you."

"Yeah, I know. I'm famous for being hit by a bus."

She was pretty accustomed to being flippant about it, calling herself a "walking metaphor," or when she couldn't remember something or got something wrong, would justify it by saying, "I get a permanent bus pass."

Five hours later—it was early afternoon when they finally wheeled us back into the pre-op room and got her prepped—a nurse arrived to check us in. "How are you?" the nurse asked.

"Okay. Am I going in soon?" Susan responded.

"Yes, sorry for the long wait. Are you nervous?" the nurse asked.

"Not that...hungry."

They assured her that it wouldn't be long, but it was still another hour or so of waiting. Finally, the anesthesiologist arrived and went through his questions, eventually asking if she'd been given anything for anxiety.

"No, but I'd like something," Susan said.

"So, you're feeling anxious?"

"Yes," she joked, "about when I'm going to get to eat again!"

Eventually she was taken in, and a few hours later Dr. Allison emerged and informed me that everything had gone very well. There was a lot of excess bone to chip away at, sort of like sculpting Mount Rushmore from a large piece of granite, but, as a result, he feels that she will have much better mobility. The bone had her completely locked up, and the knowledge he now had confirmed that all the PT in the world would never have made a difference.

Her subsequent stay in rehab was night and day compared to her first. Physical therapists, unfamiliar with Susan and used to first-timers, would come in and begin instructing her how to transfer to the wheelchair and then to stand, but Susan was way ahead of them, a seasoned expert at it all. Already, she is standing straighter than before, has far more mobility, and feels a million times better. She's no longer the hunched-over *bubbe*.

So after some quick maintenance, our rock star, the one famous for so much more than just being hit by a bus, is back on the road again...now with a bit more bounce in her limp.

day 427

There have been days that tested my patience, others that tested my strength, my resilience, faith, pretty much everything you can think of. But this one tested something altogether very different.

After Susan's latest surgery, the one thing she consciously experienced more than her previous surgeries was the pain. It was bearable, but, like every normal human being, she had to rely on painkillers to get her through the worst of it. They did the trick, but they did another trick as well. They made her extremely constipated.

She had been taking stool softeners, but to no avail, and she was getting extremely uncomfortable. So on the fourth day of this, I went to the drugstore and bought her a saline laxative. I've had to drink these for the various colonoscopies I've had, and a half a bottle was more than enough to get me going, so that's where we started.

She downed half the bottle, and we sat back and waited the ten minutes for it to kick in. After twenty minutes, there was still no action, so she drank the other half. For sure, we'd get something now, but again, after waiting twenty minutes longer, there still was nothing. This was enough laxative for a rhino, but it was having absolutely no effect.

Then the pain started. Not pain in her hip, but in her stomach, her bowels, everywhere. It was crippling, bending her over in excruciating agony for which she was desperate for relief. I had read about this kind of blockage, where it becomes so impacted that it requires going to the ER for help. I asked her if she wanted to go.

"I don't know. Yes. *Oww*. No. I don't know. Oh, my God."

I was helplessly standing by while she was writhing in pain. "What can I do?" I asked.

"Nothing. Ow. I don't know. *Owwwwww!*"

"Do you feel it coming?"

"Yes, but it's stuck. I can feel it trying to poke through, but it won't come."

She then began to breathe Lamaze-style, exhaling in bursts to deal with the pain. That is when I offered the unthinkable, the thing our vows didn't come close to covering, the true test of Dr. McSegal.

"Do you...want me to try to pull it out?"

"I don't know. Do you think you can? Whoo, whoo. Ow. *Yes!*"

I quickly ran into the hallway and found a box of surgical gloves. Slipping a pair on, I returned to the bathroom, where she was leaning against the doorframe in agony. Always the general, she commanded, "Put on some gloves!"

"I am! What do you think, I'm gonna go up there barehanded?!"

I grabbed some Vaseline and lubed the area.

"Okay, bend over," I instructed.

And then, with face scrunched and two fingers extended, I reached in. There was immediate contact.

"Can you feel it?"

"Yeah. You're right, it's stuck right at the end."

"Can you get it? Whoo, whoo, whoo," as she continued her Lamaze breathing.

"Hang on."

I pushed a little deeper, which naturally elicited another yelp of pain, and though I could feel how hard it was, it wasn't just a little nugget that was going to clear the way for the rest to follow. There was a significant mass of it.

"Okay, ready..." and then, keeping with our child-delivery motif, "Push!"

"Nnnngggg. Owwwww!"

I pulled out the first hunk, and with it cradled in my hand, I went over to the toilet and tossed it in. The immediate relief from that extraction turned Susan from being a reluctant participant into an eager one. "Oh, God, that's better. Can you get any more?"

Then the laughter started. Her tears of pain were mixed with the hilarity and embarrassment of the situation. I went back in, and for the next few minutes pulled out what I could. Soon, it was coming faster than I could keep up with, and my attempts to keep it contained to the toilet were failing as shit was basically flung around the room in our desperate attempt to clear the passageway.

We both were in hysterics, and then after a quantity that seemed like at least a couple of day's worth, she finally felt like she could do the rest on her own, and so I put her rehab commode back over the toilet and she eased herself down.

I surveyed the battle scene and began wiping up the random shrapnel, while she remained seated, blissfully evacuating amid occasional bursts of laughter. A few minutes later, I peeled off my gloves and added them to the trash bag. It was finally over.

And then, still seated there, she looked up at me, her eyes still red from laughing. "Oh, my God. That's love for you," she said, and chuckled.

You can fucking say that again.

the unposted:
part 16

Just as this entire journey has been so unpredictable, during the next few months, Susan suddenly hit another unexpected rough patch.

Though her hip surgery was successful in terms of helping with her flexibility, she began experiencing an enormous amount of pain in her leg, making it very difficult to walk. A visit back to Dr. Allison and more X-rays revealed a new complication. It turns out that even though the HO in her hip was preventing her from standing up straight, it was also protecting her femoral head (where the hip meets the thigh). Now that the HO had been removed and her hip was resting back where it should, the femoral head had begun decaying, which now required a hip replacement. The hits just kept coming.

Susan reassured me, "Love will see us through—if you don't kill me first."

This new development was hard for both of us—Susan, naturally, because she faced yet another surgery and recovery, and me, because of the demands on my patience for playing nursemaid for another post-op period. An additional complication to the whole matter, other than the medical issue, was the timing. I had taken another job by this point, one that I was much happier with. In addition to that, Alyce's bat mitzvah was coming up in a couple of weeks. After that, I had to go out of town on a shoot for ten days, followed by coming home for only a week before going back out for another ten days.

The plan was to do the surgery after the second round of filming so that I could be around for her recovery, but the pain became so intense that we had to schedule it for the week between the two shoots, hoping there'd be enough time for her to recover so that she could manage on her own while I was gone. She certainly also would be able to rely on the continued generosity and help from friends, which was comforting.

And then there was Alyce's bat mitzvah.

It's funny to think that in just one day, in fact in just a matter of hours, a boy or a girl can cross an invisible line that marks the transition from childhood to adulthood. For Alyce, at least according to the Jewish religion, that day had finally arrived.

The truth is, though this would be the day that our religion made it official, Alyce had passed over that threshold a year and a half earlier, the day that bus crossed its yellow line into the path of our car. In that instant, she dealt with facing devastating loss as she kissed her mother goodbye, thinking that it might be for forever. Pulling herself from the car, she found the presence of mind to call me. And over the next months, learned about independence, self-sufficiency, and self-sacrifice.

There was nothing about her that wasn't already a young woman. Yet, of course we were still so happy and proud to go through the formal day with her. By this point, Susan's pain was agonizing. She had tried a cortisone shot, which gave her a modicum of relief for a couple of days, but now she couldn't take a step without searing pain. Still, she wasn't going to let that interfere with this day that Alyce had worked so hard for and had been looking forward to for so long.

We were going to be back in the temple's sanctuary, by definition a place of safety and refuge, surrounded by so many who had played such significant roles over the past eighteen months. Since the accident, I'd been to my fair share of bar and bat mitzvahs. I'd let the prayer and music fill me with emotion, and the blessings and sentiments of the parents' hopes and wishes for their children push that emotion into tears. This was a holy place, but nevertheless I wondered, was it God I'd become closer to or the people who filled the space? With everything we've been through, I wasn't yet convinced that heavenly angels existed, but I was certain that human ones did.

On the day of the service, Susan rallied for the event, hiding the pain she was in. We sat in the front of the congregation, watching our girl go through the same ritual that so many millions of others have held as a defining moment in their lives. I was filled with pride, but more than that, I was incredibly grateful.

From the "parental message" I wrote for the program:

We remember when you were born, holding this little miracle in our arms. And then, over the years as you grew older and bigger, even as we continued to love you, we tended to get caught up in life and failed to remind ourselves on a daily basis of the marvel you are. And then suddenly things change, and we're once again acutely aware of this piece of grace we are blessed with. Alyce, you are that miracle of life, many times over. It's impossible to hold you and not feel grateful; impossible to not appreciate who you are and who we know you'll be as you continue life's journey."

It was a wonderful and emotional service full of a tremendous amount of love and support. As part of the service when the *bar* (boy) or *bat* (girl) mitzvah reads from the Torah, before each of these passages, the rabbi invites certain people up for an *aliyah*, which is the honor of being called to the Torah for a reading. It is meant to recognize the people most influential and close to the bar or bat mitzvah and the family. Usually, *aliyahs* consist of loved ones such as parents first, then grandparents, siblings, aunts, uncles, and cousins, but anyone can receive this honor, including teachers and friends.

For Alyce's *aliyahs*, we first called Michael up with both my mother and Susan's mother to read the Torah blessing. Fortunately, Michael was there to cover for the grandmothers, who, despite spending their entire lives as Jews and participating in Jewish events and services, and even with hours of practicing, could still only silently mouth their way through the blessing. Next came Susan and me, and after us, we brought Michael back up to the bimah.

Then, for the next *aliyah*, we did something a little different from the usual, something to recognize the gift our community had given us. The rabbi announced it: "For the third *aliyah*, the Segals would like to call you, the congregation—their family and friends—to recognize and honor the love and support you have given them. If you would all rise and, as a community, place an arm around one another as we read together the blessing."

Not only was it incredibly rewarding to give this small gift back to those who had given so much to us, but to see everyone rise and engage in this large embrace was truly special. I made a point of completely taking in the moment, standing up there with my family and looking out into our smiling, tearful community. I knew they all appreciated the miracle that we represented, standing there, the four of us, still together and fighting this ongoing battle that none of us deserved. I also knew that none of them deserved the battles they were fighting.

Everybody's got their bus. We've all been hit with something, and we deal with what we're dealt.

Following the service, that night we all gathered again for a party. While Alyce and her friends tore up the dance floor, Susan stayed confined to a chair but enjoyed herself nonetheless, talking and laughing with friends and family. It had been a wonderful day and night, and when it was over, I wheeled her back to our car and then home, where she struggled up the stairs and finally collapsed into bed.

A few days later, as the pain in her leg worsened, the time came for me to go away for my shoot; it was tough... for both of us. We had ostensibly been joined at the hip since the accident, so saying goodbye was hard enough on its own. Coupled with that, Susan was scared because she was having more and more trouble just walking, never mind taking care of the kids' needs, schlepping them around with pickups, drop-offs, baseball, softball, etc. There was also the depression of having to face yet another surgery. It was a lot to process and handle, and I, her most constant and reliable crutch, wasn't going to be around to lean on.

Thankfully, again with the help of friends, she managed okay while I was gone, but during that time, she became even more apprehensive about future potential issues and the ongoing uncertainty of what might present itself in the months and years ahead. Despite that, we continue to remind ourselves that we don't want to live that way, worrying about what *might* happen. We can only react to what does happen, and this, unfortunately, has been one of those things. In time, we'll be beyond it, and until then, all we can do is stop and remember to take in the special moments of life, basking in memories like standing up on the bimah, surrounded by so much love and joy.

day 548

It's not over yet. We're still running our race...albeit, admittedly, getting tired of it.

Susan is back in the hospital, having just emerged from a necessary hip replacement. All went as well as hoped, but because of a little more bleeding than they expected, they've decided to keep her overnight in the ICU.

So here we are, once again putting to test what has been a constant for Susan—her infinite, positive attitude. I'm confident it will remain and she will rally, digging deep to find her fourth, fifth, or eighty-fifth wind before she finally crosses that finish line.

A conventional marathon is fixed. Yes, it's twenty-six excruciating miles, but there's a beginning, middle, and an end, and at any point during it, you know where you stand. Our marathon doesn't work that way. As we run, we think, or should I say, hope, that we're finally nearing the finish line and then, like a cruel prank, it's moved forward again, just out of reach, teasing us with promised relief.

Another difference with our particular race is that, unlike conventional marathons for which there can be thousands of participants, in ours there is only one. However, we are fortunate to still have an extraordinary sideline of supporters, all cheering just for her...

To please keep running.

the unposted: part 17

I was hit (extended pause) by a bus."
    This is the statement the kids most tease Susan about, often wagering among themselves how long it will take her to make this declaration when she meets someone new. It usually isn't too long into the conversation. Being polite, people generally don't ask why she uses a cane or where the scars on her arms and neck came from or what those two little dents in her forehead are from, but when Susan has to explain why she isn't physically able to do something, like go on a college campus tour or watch everybody else ice skate from the sidelines, or is simply making conversation with someone new, she will say, "Oh, I had this crazy accident...." That's when the kids will look at each other and me, and mouth along like it's a movie they've seen a million times, "I was hit...by a bus."

    Yes, she was. At least our family maintains a sense of humor about it. Furthermore, Susan has decided to wear it as a badge of honor versus using it as an excuse or a depressing life sentence. I was hit by a bus...and I lived to tell about it.

    She says it not to garner sympathy or pity but recognizes that it *is* remarkable and should be shared with a spirit of accomplishment. It's okay to be famous for this, maybe even more so than what she grew up dreaming of becoming famous for. Because here, she actually accomplished the miraculous feat rather than simply portrayed it in a TV, theater, or movie role. She's lived it.

It's her story, not her *entire* story but certainly a significant part. She has embraced that and is determined to use it to carry her forward rather than to hold her back. And what a wonderful way to be able to walk through life, even if it's with a less-than-perfect gait.

And so, 165 days after my previous update, I posted this....

day 713: the final update

On October 23, it will be six months since Susan's hip replacement, and exactly two years since the accident. Happily, the memories of both continue to fade into the distance.

Susan is walking better than ever, more upright, still with a pronounced limp, but with no hip pain other than sore muscles after she works her body a little too hard. And that's a pain she is more welcoming of, as she knows it's a necessary and healthy part on her path to recovery.

As we approach the two-year mark, it really feels like we're coming to the end. There will naturally be other challenges ahead, but hopefully they will be the kind we'll consider ourselves lucky to face—Michael soon going off to college, Alyce entering high school, decisions about our future that are no longer centered around the events of the past two years. Throughout this entire journey, the one enduring hope from us and from all of you is that we somehow, at some time, emerge on the other side of this. Thankfully, it feels like we are at last there.

With that in mind, we did something the kids have been begging us to do since they were little and that Susan's delusions prophesied—we got a dog! He's a rescue, curly hair, fashionably black with little white socks for feet and white around his neck. When we first took him out on his leash, I noticed that he also walked a little sideways. It turns out he had been hit by a car and had to have a plate surgically inserted into his hip. When the kids heard this, noting the uncanny similarities of his injury as well as his curly hair and stylish black outfit, they said, "Mom, we got *you* as a dog!" Bruce (that's his name) also doesn't wallow in his injury. He isn't lamenting; his spirit is purely positive. He's just gotten on with his life, is happy to see us when we return home from our days, happy to play...just happy. Those qualities are quintessentially Susan.

And so it's natural to wonder, and a question the whole family has been asked, "How has this entire experience affected you?" For me, some of that answer is contained in the many entries that came before this. For Susan and the kids, despite it being two years, some of the answer may be too early to tell.

In fact, on occasion, we discuss such questions among our-selves. For example, yesterday while we were all driving home, Mi-chael asked, "How do you think the whole experience affected the way you parented us?" I explained that I didn't want to drag them onto the emotional roller coaster of good days and bad days, and that I tried to protect them from that. I also told them that I tried to normalize things at home as much as possible, by continuing to take them to school and to be home to share dinners together like before the accident.

Many assumed that I camped out in the hospital that first night and every night for the duration of Susan's stay, curled in a reclin-ing hospital chair with a limp blanket, surrounded by the sounds of the ICU machines and moans and coughs from the patients and electronic honks from the ventilators. The truth is, I didn't stay over-night in the hospital that first night, or any night. My decision might have been different had we lived farther than fifteen minutes away from the hospital. I knew I could get there quickly if I needed to, and I wanted to be home with the kids. Each in their own way was experiencing the worst time in their life, and if they couldn't have their mom, I wanted them to have their dad. Susan was uncon-scious and surrounded by the finest doctors and nurses. She might have sensed my presence in the room or subconsciously known I was there, but I knew she didn't need me to be there to know that I loved her and was sending my strength. On the other hand, I felt my kids did.

So I was home with them for dinners and intent on maintaining a sense of normalcy, but it was still far from normal. Alyce refers to those first few weeks as being like living in a horror movie, and the phone was the murderer. Over dinner, they'd sit and pray it didn't ring. Periods of quiet would cause the suspense to build in the same way a killer lurks nearby, threatening to burst in at any moment.

And then, on occasion, it *would* ring, causing our hearts to leap. They'd watch fearfully as I'd go to answer it, approaching it like a helpless victim approaches a closed door to check what's outside, while my kids silently screamed, "Don't answer it!" afraid of what was going to leap out at us. The news we were all terrified of hear-ing lived on the other side of that phone line, and we never knew if or when it was going to strike.

This was the state we lived in for some time, lulled at times into thinking everything was safe and good, only to be jolted back into the fear of it all with a new complication or piece of news. But we always had one another for comfort, and hopefully the kids' injuries, like Susan's, will continue to heal, theirs without permanent scars.

Another question I'm often asked is, "How has the accident affected you...spiritually speaking?"

This one is a little more complicated. Not that I have an antagonistic relationship or feel hurt or betrayed by God. In fact, I'm not even sure I've *had* a relationship with God. I definitely have had a fear, like if I do something bad or wrong or speak ill about Him/Her, that I might pay a terrible consequence, but does that qualify as a relationship? Feels more like a superstition. And if it is a relationship, it certainly doesn't sound like the most healthy of ones. All that said, I also have never had the thought, *God, what did I, or we, do to deserve this?* partly because I know we didn't say or do anything to bring this upon ourselves, and partly because I don't believe that God had any hand in causing the accident at all.

What about surviving it, though? After Susan got out of the hospital, a friend called her, one who claims to have psychic abilities. She told Susan that on the day of the accident, she had a very strong vision and from it knew that Susan was ultimately going to survive. She clearly saw the accident and saw Susan's spirit connected to this earth by what resembled an umbilical cord. The cord hadn't been severed, which is how the friend knew she was going to live. She also saw that at the scene of the accident there were "many angels" helping her. Susan's father was helping to pull the car away from under the bus, but it was too heavy and he needed help, from which the psychic said Susan's brother gave him. She asked if Susan had a brother who had passed and Susan answered, "Well, a brother-in-law." The friend then said that he must have been the one helping. She also told Susan that her grandmother (who had always complimented Susan on how pretty she was) had protected her face. From the accident, with all the injuries Susan sustained, her face was relatively unharmed, except for a burn on her chin from the air bag.

Was this reported vision an uncanny coincidence or a glimpse into another dimension that most of us don't have access to? I don't know. The afterlife is one phenomenon I'd really like to believe in—and there are many others. I've worked on television shows centered around UFOs and aliens, and while I've heard some pretty compelling stories about their existence, I've never actually seen or experienced one, so it's difficult to believe completely. UFOs, aliens, the afterlife...they all fall into the same category of wanting to believe but needing more proof. Some believe that children are more susceptible to seeing ghosts and other paranormal phenomena because their minds are more open. So I wonder, with the innocence of my own childhood behind me, is it my closed mind preventing me from seeing what is already right in front of me?

Like the existence of God.

When Susan was first in the hospital and able to start processing what had happened to her, I told her a little about her journey thus far. By this time, she knew she had been in a car accident and was at Cedars-Sinai Medical Center. And on this particular day, I also told her that when she was in the midst of all her initial surgeries, the head of Cedars' orthopedic surgery department had been watching over her case. I explained that our anesthesiologist friend at the Hospital for Special Surgery in New York had spoken to his boss there, who knew the head of orthopedic surgery at Cedars, and that's how he became involved. Susan had a tracheostomy at the time that I told her all of this, and she was only able to scratch out a few words. "Really? That's sweet."

"Yes, you have a lot of angels watching over you," I added.

Partly because her case was so unique, but also from the many connections we had either through friends or work, it was true. We did have a lot of angels watching over her.

A week or so later, one of the rabbis from our temple, Michelle, called me. She was at Cedars visiting her uncle, who had been admitted around the same time as Susan and was wondering if she could come and say hello to her. I told her I wasn't there at the moment, but if Susan were awake, I'm sure she would love to see her. I gave her the building and room number and hung up. An hour or so later my phone rang, and it was Rabbi Michelle again. She said that she had indeed seen Susan and had such an extraordinary visit with her that she had to call and share it with me. She said that she had been talking to Susan about how wonderful it was to see her doing so well, what a blessing it was that she was still here. Susan had smiled, and in the haze that she was in, this is what she told Michelle (by the way, Susan doesn't remember having this conversation with Michelle at all):

Susan told her that she believed that one of the reasons she had survived was because of the many connections she had in Sinai. Michelle was thrown by this, naturally thinking of the biblical Mount Sinai where God gave the Ten Commandments to Moses. "Sinai? Really?" Michelle asked.

When she asked her what she meant by this, Susan responded, "There are a lot of angels watching over me."

"Where have you seen these angels?" Michelle asked.

"Oh, around...in the operating room, you know."

"And what did these angels do?"

"They would just lean in and give me hugs," Susan said.

This is the perfect illustration of my spiritual dilemma, the battle between heart and head. Through Rabbi Michelle's lens, the heart, this was an extraordinary affirmation of her faith—ancient connections in Sinai, angels watching over us giving us strength and love. Through my lens, the head, it was how information previously given to Susan had been mentally processed—slightly twisted and then repeated.

Belief versus skepticism. The truth is, they both live in me.

Like many, I so want to believe in God without a shadow of doubt, but my rational mind often comes into battle with that pure faith. I look for empirical proof. I'm sure many of you are thinking, *My God, how much more proof do you need than what you've already been shown?!* Admittedly, there is some truth in just that. There's an old joke about a holy man who is caught in a torrential rain that turns into a flood. As the water is rising and up to his knees, a raft comes by to rescue him. He turns the raft away and says, "Go rescue someone else. God will save me." A little later, the water is up to his chest, and a boat comes by. He turns the boat away, saying that God will save him. Later, when the water is up to his neck, a helicopter arrives and he turns that away, too, shouting up to it, "God will save me!" It continues to rain and the water continues to rise until it is now over his head, and the man drowns. He finds himself in heaven and approaches God, pretty pissed off. "God, I don't understand how you could do this to me? I have served you my entire life. I had complete faith in you and yet you turned your back on me when I needed you most." God says, "What are you talking about? I sent you a raft. I sent you a boat. I even sent you a helicopter.

when I think of it, had I prayed, what would I have asked God to provide? Strength, comfort, something to help bear the weight, a presence to vent to...support. Well, that's exactly what I received...but
from people like you, some family, some friends, some complete
strangers. Countless emails of love and hope, shoulders to cry on,
encouragement—all of it life-sustaining nourishment. The words I
wrote that I never considered prayer ultimately became the best
example of the power of prayer. And while we have often heard the
phrase that God is within all of us, I would go further and say that
God isn't *within* all of us; God *is* all of us. We all have the power, the
heart, the compassion, the resources to provide one another with
exactly what many turn to God for. And I say this not based on faith
but entirely on observation and experience. As Susan always says,
love really is the answer.

And while there are times when Susan has uttered the words,
"Why did this have to happen?" she has never once said, "Why did
this have to happen to *me*?" She has refused to be a victim, and it is
this attitude that has kept her from wallowing in self-pity. Her zest
for life, her spirit, and lack of fatalism are just some of the many
characteristics that have helped in her survival and healing. Without these qualities, the ones that live in us all, I'm not sure what her
outcome would have been.

She continues to carry the accident with her—in the scars, the
numbness from the nerve damage, the aches and pains, the lost
time...her bag of rocks to bear. Each of us has been saddled with
a bag of rocks. And what I also know to be true is that, together,
we can help one another carry them. The inspiration, strength, and
hope Susan has provided has helped others carry theirs. And the
love she's received has helped carry hers. The kind words back to
me, as well as all the support, have helped me carry mine.

I'm not sure, even given the choice, whether I'd want to live
without life's heavy weights. The greater the pain we allow ourselves to feel, the greater the joy we can experience in return, spik-
ing up and down like the EKG of a heart. Limit the pain and we limit
the joy, compressing the lines closer and closer, flatter and flatter.
Without the up-and-down spikes of life's heartaches and elations,
like an EKG in flatline, we cease to live.

So here we are today, nearly two years after this journey began. Susan continues to improve, the kids are thriving, and this I

do know for sure: Through reaching out with these words, all my prayers have been answered.

I don't need any more proof than that.

epilogue

That, indeed, was the final update.

It wasn't that we'd reached the end. Actually, it was quite the contrary. With the passage of time came the realization that the marathon we continued to run was no different from the everyday marathon of life, each day bringing a new challenge, a new setback, while also bringing much forward progress, growth, satisfaction, and happiness. We knew that things would never return to what they had been before the accident, but when does that ever happen in life? With each passing day, we are never quite the same, and through accepting that comes a sense of liberation. We were no longer anticipating a certain result and disappointed when it didn't arrive. We would, and will, just take it as it comes. This was our lot in life, and all in all, despite its flaws, we were blessed to have it.

Susan's biggest concern coming out of all of this is that she's going to become old before her time—achy, arthritic, physically limited. Early on in her rehab, she came home from a water aerobics class she tried at the Y. When I asked her how it went, she said, "Well, let's just say, it was a far cry from SoulCycle. I was the youngest. The instructor was ninety-three, and for the first exercise, she accompanied her leg lifts by singing, 'Daisy, Daisy, give me your answer do...'

"And on top of that, I had to fight an old Russian lady."

I paused, because though it's been a long time since her delusions, this sounded suspiciously reminiscent of her escapades with the octopus. Now she's fighting an old Russian lady? So she told me what had happened:

When she got into the pool, she moved to the front to be closer to the instructor and apparently had inadvertently taken this old Russian woman's spot.

"You must move over there," the Russian said in her thick accent, trying to bully Susan.

"Um, no I don't," Susan responded.

The woman took a beat, taking Susan in. "You were one hit by bus, yes?" (Yes, famous even at the Y.)

"That's me," Susan admitted.

The old Russian considered that for another few seconds, nodded, and then decided to give Susan her space.

And that has been one constant throughout all of this. It's hard not to respect someone who has gone through something like this and is still out there fighting the fight. Many others would have seen that ninety-three-year-old water aerobics teacher and the elderly class takers and become so depressed that they quit the class. Not Susan. She recognized that that's where she was at with her recovery for the moment, and returned to the class the following day. She knows that there's still a ways to go, and that's going to require continued work. As my doctor says, "It's a lot easier to stay healthy than it is to get healthy."

The one thing we did go through, not injury related but difficult for both of us and especially for Susan, was that we ended up having to sell our house. The bills and debt just became too much. We also needed a high school for Alyce, and moving allowed her to go to a great public school on the westside, where we relocated.

Susan, however, took the move very hard. Not only did

she love our house—we both did—but I think that for so long it represented the place she was desperate to get back to, physically from the hospital and emotionally as a place she was proud of, where she entertained her friends, where her family was. It was home, and having to leave it was sad, and many tears were shed. I tried to comfort her by saying that it was only a house and that our friends were still our friends and more importantly, our family was still together. We're amazingly lucky that the only thing we ended up mourning is our house. She intellectually understood all of that, but it still represented a big loss.

We get attached to these things, and, as we all know, change can be hard and scary. I heard someone say, "The scarier change is, the more we probably need it," but I don't know if I completely subscribe to that. When things are good, we want them to stay that way. The problem with change is that most of the time we don't choose it. We're *forced* into change, so we naturally resist it rather than embrace it as the next chapter in our lives. This was one of those cases, and I could only hope and have faith that, like so many other life experiences, with time and retrospect, we would see that this change, too, was good and perhaps even meant to be.

There are so many other stories from this experience I haven't included that illustrate the various lives that were touched by the accident—the school event for Alyce when a woman came running up to Susan and said, "I just had to introduce myself. I was one of your doctors in the ER!" Or when another came running across the grocery store parking lot and said, "I was your nurse in the ICU!"

There was also our annual block party that we held in front of our house. We always invited the fire department to come so that the kids could climb onto the fire engine and meet the firefighters. As Susan milled about, happily reconnecting with our neighbors, one of our friends came over to her and said, "Oh, my God. You have to come say hello to the firemen. Their engine was the first responder to your accident!" They were unbelievably happy to meet Susan. They had seen the damage to the car. They were the ones who cut her out of the vehicle, but never heard whether she had survived or not, and frankly didn't think she would. And here they were, a year later, meeting the living example of their efforts. It was a reward they don't often get to experience, rarely learning the ultimate fate of their rescue efforts.

When I think about some of these stories, it's fascinating how many of them fall into the "small world" category. But there is one story that stretches the idea of a "small world" coincidence into something beyond categorizing. It begins at the scene of the accident:

Alyce remembers getting out of the car and needing to call me, but her backpack with her phone was still trapped inside the crushed vehicle. While standing outside in shock and crying, she remembers a woman approaching her in a bathrobe and comforting her. She loaned Alyce her cell phone to call me. I didn't meet this woman, but I'd saved the number that had come up on the caller ID on a little scrap of paper, intending to call her back and thank her. It was a few weeks after the accident when I finally got around to it, but instead of a woman answering the phone, a man did, and he didn't really know what I was talking about. He wasn't aware of the accident but said that maybe his wife had his phone at the time and that perhaps she had helped Alyce. I said, "Well, please thank her for me if it was her. I am so grateful for her help." He said he would, and that was the end of it.

More than two years later, we were at an event at our synagogue celebrating Martin Luther King Jr. and the fifty-year anniversary of his speaking there. It was a night that embraced racial and cultural diversity as well as unity and commonalities that bind us together. It was a look back at how far we've come in the past fifty years, but also, in too many ways, the short distance we've actually traveled. The message pouring from every speaker that night was that the cure for the disease that still plagues much of the world, racism, was simply "love," which of course spoke to Susan and her journey. She continues to credit her survival and recovery to the miracle healing power of love.

Before the event began, however, our temple's cantor and musical director, Danny, rushed up to us. He excitedly approached us and said, "There's a woman here tonight from one of the church choirs who you have to meet!" Apparently, while rehearsing that evening for the performance, the woman had approached him and said, "You know, there was an accident a couple of years ago very near this temple." Danny responded that, yes, he was familiar with the accident and informed her that the woman and young girl involved in it were temple members. The woman then apprehensively asked him if she had survived, knowing how awful the wreck was. Danny happily answered, "Yes, in fact, I'm quite confident she'll be here tonight."

The woman was clearly overcome with emotion finding out the miraculous outcome and revealed to Danny that she was at the scene, had helped the little girl who was in the car, and knew that *she* was okay but never found out about the driver. Danny told her that he would be sure to introduce us after the event.

At the reception following the event, we found Danny, who initially, among the large crowd, couldn't find the woman. As the night wore on and the crowd thinned, Danny finally approached us, an African-American woman with a bright, glowing smile by his side. He turned to the woman and then to us and said, "I want to introduce you to Susan."

Having heard Danny's story earlier, Susan immediately

knew who this woman was and the two embraced warmly, tears filling their eyes. The woman then told us her version of the story. She had seen Alyce standing by the side of the wrecked car, visibly upset, and approached her, asking, "Is that your mom in there?" Alyce nodded that it was, and seeing the devastation of the accident, the woman said to her, "Let's pray together." Sweet, innocent Alyce looked at this woman wearing a prominent cross around her neck and responded, "Okay, but you should know...I'm Jewish." The woman smiled, took Alyce's hand, then held it to her chest and said, "That's okay. In here, we're all the same."

The fact that this story was being told on MLK's birthday was not lost on any of us.

I told the woman that I had tried to reach her to thank her for helping Alyce. I asked her if she ever received the message from her husband. She was confused and said she hadn't. When I explained that I had called a few weeks after the accident, she told me that she had gotten rid of that cell phone and been assigned a new phone number. But she was sorry she didn't get the call because she and her entire building had prayed for Susan. They, too, would be so happy to hear that she survived.

This wasn't the first time I'd heard of total strangers praying on Susan's behalf. I'd received emails from friends from all over the country and the world asking if it would be okay if their various churches from every denomination held us in their prayers. Through a Buddhist couple and their connections, we even had a thousand Tibetan monks praying for Susan's recovery. Tragedy is blind to religion, and we were grateful to be on the receiving end of these universal prayers.

We had our picture taken together, and as we were saying goodbye, she again warmly hugged Susan and then me. We realized we had never been formally introduced, so she said to me, "I'm sorry, I never got your name." I told her it was Doug, and she paused, a little confused, like maybe she hadn't heard me. I repeated it, "Doug, like Douglas."

She then looked at us and said, "Wait, your name is Susan?" Susan nodded yes. "And your name is Douglas?" She then put her hand over her heart and said, "Oh, my goodness. *My* name is Susan Douglas."

The coincidence was heart-stopping. This angel happened to live in the apartment building right where the accident occurred, had taken care of Alyce, had prayed with her for this stranger in a crushed car, and had continued to pray along with residents of her apartment complex, and her name was Susan Douglas.

At one of the past High Holiday services, the rabbi asked everyone who had experienced a *simcha*, something positive in their life, to please come up and be part of a special blessing. A number of people began to make their way toward the front, and I encouraged Susan to join them. Initially, she was reluctant but eventually relented. While up there, the rabbi passed around a microphone, asking to hear the particular circumstances people were grateful for. Some were grateful for a new grandchild, a new job or promotion, even a divorce.

And then it reached Susan, who when handed the mic and asked what she was grateful for, simply leaned into it and said, "I'm alive?" It had a little question mark of inflection at the end of it, like asking, "Do I have to have more than that?" The roar of applause for that simple sentiment of gratitude was a reminder for everyone in the room.

No, you don't have to have any more than that.

Is that simply what we are meant to get from all of this? I remember one particular day, months after the accident, Susan was in the hospital's radiology room for yet another set of X-rays, and the technician checked his paper to see what images were to be taken. Seeing the absurdly high number, he turned to her and said, "Wow, is there anything you didn't break?" The answer was, "No, not really." He then added, "Well, I guess you're still here for a reason."

Comments like this always struck an uncomfortable chord with Susan, trying to somehow justify this random event with some bigger purpose in life she was yet to fulfill. She turned to the technician, not angrily, but like him, just trying to make some deeper sense of this. "What is this big purpose I suddenly need to have? I liked my life. I was happy with my career. I have a husband I love, two beautiful children, a lovely home, wonderful friends. What am I supposed to do now, solve world peace?"

The technician wasn't put off but rather stopped his preparations, looked at her, and smiled warmly. He then asked, "Has your story inspired anyone?"

"I don't know. I suppose it has," she responded.

"Well, maybe that's it. If your story can inspire just one person, then that's reason enough for being here."

And that is ultimately why we tell it.

I used to joke that the tear-jerky Hollywood ending to this story, after everything we've gone through, is that either Susan or I die. Having heard my fair share of studio feedback on potential movie projects, I can easily imagine the note: "I love it! Super compelling. But let me ask you, would it be possible for one of them to, you know, *die* in the end? That would be beautiful. Perfectly and tragically heartbreaking."

But this story isn't about the tragedy of dying. It's about the everyday challenge of living, and how we get over and through our collective hardships. Dying doesn't require much effort. It's living, surviving, and recovering that test us.

After Susan and Alyce got struck that day, we as a family have been struck by a number of things. Among them, the healing power of love and compassion, the resilience of humans, the randomness of life. Whenever Susan and I are at a party or gathering, people still tell her that simply seeing her brings a smile to their face, just being reminded of the miracle that she's still here, reminded that in an instant, at any time, life can turn on a dime.

When I was in college and living in New York City, there was a news story about someone who got hit in the head and killed by a brick that fell off of a construction site. With all the scaffolding I walked under on a daily basis, that easily could have been my brick, my head. Living in fear of that is surely unhealthy and can be debilitating, but there's a balance to be found knowing that, even though it's unlikely, it's still a possibility. An awareness of all the random acts of tragedy that populate today's world demands a sense of appreciation and gratefulness when they don't fall upon us.

Because they happen every day.

Last year, Susan and I planned a trip to take the kids to Paris over Thanksgiving. A week before we were set to leave, the terrorist attack at the Bataclan theater occurred. We were nervous about going but ultimately decided not to cancel. In the London airport, while we were transferring to our flight to Paris, we began a conversation with two women who were headed back home to Ireland. When they asked us where we were going, we hesitantly said, "Paris."

They looked at us and instead of telling us we were crazy, like many in the States had, they smiled, nodded, and said, "Good for you for going on with it." And then with their lilting accents, they added, "Terrible what happened, and a great reminder...we have to live for today because you never know...tomorrow you might get hit by a bus."

Susan and I shared a look and smiled, knowing all too well, for even though the saying might be a cliché...

The truth is, we should, because we absolutely might.

acknowledgments

First, a big thank-you to everyone at Prospect Park Books, including Dorie Bailey, Caitlin Ek, Margery Schwartz, Leilah Bernstein, Amy Inouye, cover designer David Ter-Avanyesan, and especially Colleen Dunn Bates for embracing the book so enthusiastically. Also, thanks to Christopher Noxon for the introduction. Deep appreciation goes to Susan's core group and book club for their love, support, and early reads: Tracy Miller, Linda Brettler, Alexa Pogue, Nancy Ortenberg, Jode Mann, Erica Huggins, Christine Bubser, Jacqui Biery, Ariane Bushkin, Lisa Angel, Jen DeVore, Deedee Atkinson, Maddie Moskowitz, Ruthie Jones, Caroline Andoscia, Gina Belafonte, Karen Ray, and a special thank-you to Kabrel Geller, the original gatekeeper of the updates. Also, enormous love to Charles and Karen Spencer, Debra Zakarin, Dana Stevens, Julie Graham, Mitch Marcus, Elisabeth Rudolph, and Geoffrey Nauffts for their guidance and wisdom.

To all the many lifesavers, including the staff at Cedars-Sinai, particularly Dr. Daniel Allison, Dr. Eli Baron, Dr. Nicolas Melo, Dr. Eric Ley, Dr. Gregory Hallert, Dr. Rex Chung, Dr. Daniel Margulies, Dr. Rebecca Hedrick, Dr. Jeffrey Wertheimer, Dr. Anne Meyer, Esther Morrison, everyone in the ER, the nurses and physical therapists, especially Rand, LAFD Engine #41, all the first responders, Inez Beltran at MPIHIP, and BMW for making a car that could withstand a bus.

The clergy at Temple Israel of Hollywood, including